GREAT MYSTERIES

The Trojan War

OPPOSING VIEWPOINTS®

Look for these and other exciting *Great Mysteries: Opposing Viewpoints* books:

Amelia Earhart *by Jane Leder*
Anastasia, Czarina or Fake?
   by Leslie McGuire
Animal Communication *by Jacci Cole*
The Assassination of President Kennedy
   by Jeffrey Waggoner
Atlantis *by Wendy Stein*
The Beginning of Language
   by Clarice Swisher
The Bermuda Triangle *by Norma Gaffron*
Bigfoot *by Norma Gaffron*
Dinosaurs *by Peter & Connie Roop*
The Discovery of America
   by Renardo Barden
ESP *by Michael Arvey*
The Loch Ness Monster *by Robert San Souci*
Noah's Ark *by Patricia Kite*
Pearl Harbor *by Deborah Bachrach*
Poltergeists *by Peter & Connie Roop*
Pyramids *by Barbara Mitchell*
Reincarnation *by Michael Arvey*
The Shroud of Turin *by Daniel C. Scavone*
The Solar System *by Peter & Connie Roop*
Stonehenge *by Peter & Connie Roop*
The Trojan War *by Gail Stewart*
UFOs *by Michael Arvey*
Unicorns *by Norma Gaffron*
Witches *by Bryna Stevens*

GREAT MYSTERIES

The Trojan War

OPPOSING VIEWPOINTS®

by Gail Stewart

Greenhaven Press, Inc.   P.O. Box 289009, San Diego, California 92128-9009

Library of Congress Cataloging-in-Publication Data

Stewart, Gail, 1949-
    The Trojan War / by Gail Stewart.
      p.   cm. — (Great mysteries : opposing viewpoints)
    Bibliography: p.
    Includes index.
    Summary: Explores the mystery surrounding the occurrence, location, and heroes of the Trojan War.
    ISBN 0-89908-065-0
    1. Troy (Ancient city)—Juvenile literature. 2. Trojan War—Juvenile literature. 3. Turkey—Antiquities—Juvenile literature.
[1. Troy (Ancient city) 2. Trojan War. 3. Turkey—Antiquities.]
I. Title. II. Series: Great mysteries (Saint Paul, Minn.)
DF221.T8S65 1989
939'.21—dc20   89-11616
                                             CIP
                                             AC

*For my family, Carl, Ted,
Elliot, and Flynn Arrow*

"When men and women lose the sense of mystery, life will prove to be a gray and dreary business, only with difficulty to be endured."

Harold T. Wilkins, author of Strange Mysteries of Time and Space

Contents

	Introduction	9
Preface	A Mighty Battle	10
One	Did the Trojan War Really Happen?	14
Two	Who Could Solve the Mystery of Troy?	26
Three	Was Troy at Hissarlik?	42
Four	What Was the Connection with Mycenae?	56
Five	Who Were the Mycenaeans?	70
Six	Was Homer's Story True?	88
Seven	What Happened to the Heroic Age?	98
Epilogue	The Search Continues	104
	Books for Further Exploration	107
	Index	109
	Picture Credits	111
	About the Author	112

Introduction

This book is written for the curious—those who want to explore the mysteries that are everywhere. To be human is to be constantly surrounded by wonderment. How do birds fly? Are ghosts real? Can animals and people communicate? Was King Arthur a real person or a myth? Why did Amelia Earhart disappear? Did history really happen the way we think it did? Where did the world come from? Where is it going?

Great Mysteries: Opposing Viewpoints books are intended to offer the reader an opportunity to explore some of the many mysteries that both trouble and intrigue us. For the span of each book, we want the reader to feel that he or she is a scientist investigating the extinction of the dinosaurs, an archaeologist searching for clues to the origin of the great Egyptian pyramids, a psychic detective testing the existence of ESP.

One thing all mysteries have in common is that there is no ready answer. Often there are *many* answers but none on which even the majority of authorities agrees. *Great Mysteries: Opposing Viewpoints* books introduce the intriguing views of the experts, allowing the reader to participate in their explorations, their theories, and their disagreements as they try to explain the mysteries of our world.

But most readers won't want to stop here. These *Great Mysteries: Opposing Viewpoints* aim to stimulate the reader's curiosity. Although truth is often impossible to discover, the search is fascinating. It is up to the reader to examine the evidence, to decide whether the answer is there—or to explore further.

"Penetrating so many secrets, we cease to believe in the unknowable. But there it sits nevertheless, calmly licking its chops."
H.L. Mencken, American essayist

Preface

A Mighty Battle

Long ago, more than one thousand years before Christ, two armies were at war. They were fighting near a large city called Troy, in a land that is now called Turkey. The war had been going on for almost ten years, and although thousands of men had been killed, the fighting showed no sign of slowing down.

The invading Greek army had been trying to overcome the mighty city of Troy, but the Trojan army held them back. If only they could get past the tall outer walls of the city, the Greeks knew, they had a chance of overpowering the Trojans and ending the war. But the walls were sturdy and high, and armed Trojan sentries kept watch from towers day and night.

Finally one of the Greeks had a plan that would get at least a few of them inside the Trojan walls. They would build a huge wooden horse with a hollow belly in which several armed men could hide. The horse would be left as a sort of peace offering to the Trojans. The Greeks would burn their camp, get into their ships, and sail away. This would give the Trojans the impression that the Greeks were giving up and going home.

This medieval French enamel depicts the Trojan war. The soldiers are dressed as they would have been in medieval times (about 500 years ago) instead of during the time of the Trojans (more than 2500 years ago).

> "Sing the building of the wooden horse, made by Epeis with Athena's aid, which royal Odysseus once conveyed into the Trojan citadel—a thing of craft, filled full of men, who by its means sacked Troy."
>
> A passage from the *Odyssey*

> "Anyone who doesn't think the Trojans were utterly stupid will have realised that the horse was really an engineer's device for breaking down the walls."
>
> Second-century Greek historian Pausanias, quoted in *In Search of the Trojan War*

The plan was a good one. The Trojans, seeing the empty harbor and the abandoned Greek camp, were elated. Surely the gods and goddesses were smiling down on the brave city of Troy! And such a peace offering left by the retreating Greeks!

They pulled the gigantic wooden horse inside the walls of the city and began a feast to celebrate their victory. Late into the night the party continued, until the exhausted Trojans sank into sleep. They did not hear the trap door in the belly of the horse slide open, or the handful of Greek soldiers ease themselves out of their cramped hiding place. They did not notice that the Greek ships had sailed back to the shore and were silently waiting under the full moon for a signal.

Once out of the horse, the Greeks quietly killed the sentries and unlocked the gates of the city. They lit a signal fire for the awaiting army. The scene that followed was bloody.

This engraving, based on a painting by Henri Motte, shows a very majestic Trojan horse.

Finally inside the walls of the city, the Greek army was like a killing machine, slaughtering every Trojan man and boy they could find. Most of the women and girls were taken hostage and led away to the Greek ships. They would be divided up among the warriors later and used as slaves. When the night was over, Troy was a blazing ruin and its inhabitants were either prisoners or dead.

This engraving depicts the legend of the Laocoön, a priest killed with his sons by two sea serpents after they warned the Trojans against the wooden horse.

One

Did the Trojan War Really Happen?

That was the final episode in what is perhaps the most famous war in history. The tale of Troy has been told and written about for thousands of years. Scores of legends and myths have grown up around the tale, many of them contradictory.

Most of what we know of the Trojan War comes from an ancient Greek poet named Homer. He is credited with composing two great poems about the war and its aftermath. The first of these poems, the *Iliad*, is named for Ilium, which is another name for the city of Troy. The *Iliad* concerns itself with events in the final year of the war, and especially with the death of Hector, one of the bravest Trojan warriors. The *Odyssey*, the second of Homer's famous poems, tells the story of Odysseus, a Greek hero. Odysseus had unknowingly offended one of the gods. As punishment, his journey home after the war was long and dangerous.

Very little is known about Homer himself. From studying the language and style of his storytelling, historians believe he lived sometime in the eighth or ninth centuries B.C. No one knows precisely where in Greece he lived. But today, seven cities claim to be his birthplace!

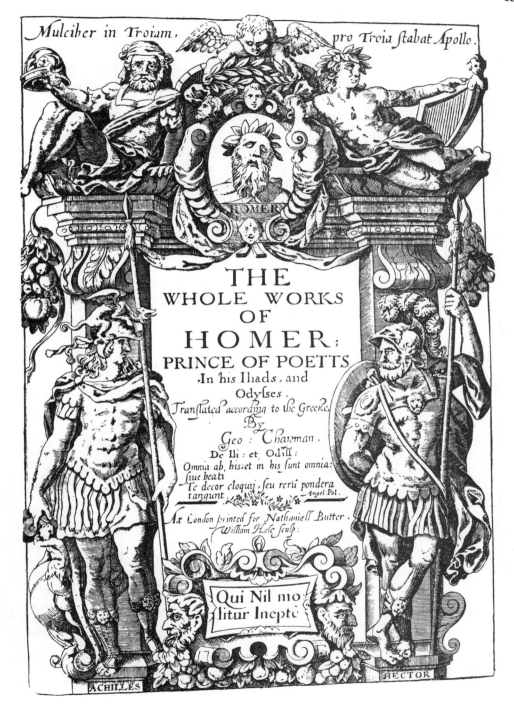

Mulciber in Troiam,   pro Troia stabat Apollo.

HOMER

THE
WHOLE WORKS
OF
HOMER;
PRINCE OF POETTS

In his Iliads, and
Odysses.
Translated according to the Greeke,
By
Geo: Chapman.
De Ili: et. Odill:
Omnia ab, his:et in his sunt omnia:
siue beati
Te decor eloquij, seu rerii pondera
tangunt.   Angel:Pol.

At London printed for Nathaniell Butter.
William Hole sculp:

Qui Nil mo
litur Inepte

ACHILLES   HECTOR

Early	Eastern	Western	Classical
A	A	A	A
B	B	B	B
Λ	Λ	Λ	Γ
Δ	Δ	Δ	Δ
E	E	E	E
﹂			
I	I	I	Z
B	B		H
⊗	⊙	⊙	θ
⟨	I	I	I
𐤊	Ϝ	K	K
⟨	⟨	⟨	Λ
M	M	M	M
Ͷ	N	N	N
	Ξ		Ξ
O	O	O	O
Π	Γ	Γ	Π
M			
ϙ	Q	Q	
ꟼ	P	P	P
S	⟨	S	Σ
X	T	T	T
	Y	Y	Y
	X	X+	X

Four versions of the Greek alphabet.

If the scholars have correctly dated his poems, then Homer was alive at the time Greek history officially "began." The eighth century B.C. was when the ancient Greeks adopted an alphabet and began keeping written records. Everything prior to this time is considered "prehistoric"—that is, before written history. All that was known about the past was passed from one generation to the next orally; important events were kept alive by storytellers.

Historians such as Milman Parry and Albert Lord have done extensive research confirming what earlier historians had suspected; that Homer was an oral poet—that is, he did not write down his poetry. (It is important to understand that although Homer was probably alive at the time the alphabet was being used for the first time in Greece, writing would not have been used by poets. The earliest uses of the alphabet were for government record keeping. A handful of palace scribes were most likely the only ones who could read and write at first.)

A Greek *rhapsodos*, or "singer." These people entertained by reciting poetry at festivals, thereby keeping Homer's epic tales and other oral literature alive.

The *Iliad* and the *Odyssey* were sung or recited perhaps with the musical accompaniment of a harp or lyre. The poems were passed down from one oral poet to another for generations. Later, perhaps not for a century or more, the poems were finally written down. The earliest written manuscripts of the *Iliad* that still exist today date back to the tenth century A.D., although ancient writers, including the Roman Cicero, referred to a written version of Homer's poems existing in 550 B.C. Undoubtedly many valuable documents have been lost in the passing of centuries.

The siege of Troy was not, as Homer points out, something that happened in his lifetime, nor did it happen in the lifetimes of his parents, or even his grandparents. Rather, he narrates stories and events that must have happened centuries before, if at all. Since Homer had no written documents to draw from, he must have depended on the strong oral tradition for the story of the Trojan War.

"The Most Famous War Ever Fought"

One of the best-known legends about the cause of the Trojan War comes not from Homer's version of the war, but from a later myth. It tells of a wedding to which the goddess of strife, Eris, was not invited. Eager to cause trouble at the event, she threw a beautiful golden apple down among the guests. The apple was to be a prize for the most beautiful goddess of them all. Naturally there was a dispute, in this case among three goddesses. Hera, the queen of the gods, Aphrodite, the goddess of love, and Athena, the goddess of wisdom, were each convinced that the apple should be hers.

None of the gods wanted to risk acting as a judge in this beauty contest, so it was decided that they would find an unbiased young man to make the judgment. Paris, the son of the Trojan king Priam, was chosen. He was approached by each of the three goddesses. He was a handsome young man, and the god-

"Our evidence has shown that the seizure of women on overseas raids was indeed a common feature of this world, and the more beautiful the better. Of Helen we can at least conclude that she is possible!"

Author Michael Wood, *In Search of the Trojan War*

"The city was admirably placed to levy tolls upon vessels wishing to pass through the Hellespont. . . . Perhaps it was this, and not Helen's face, that launched a thousand ships upon Ilium."

Author Will Durant, *The Life of Greece*

King Menelaus and his wife Helen, as depicted on a Greek vase. Supposedly, Helen's great beauty was the cause of the ten-year Trojan War.

The goddesses Hera, Athena, and Aphrodite, and Zeus, the king of the gods. Paris, the young mortal, was forced to choose the most beautiful of these goddesses.

desses tried their best to win his favor. Hera offered to make him the richest man in the world. Athena offered him the gifts of wisdom and understanding beyond that of any other mortal. Aphrodite promised him the most beautiful woman in the world. According to the legends, Paris did not even hesitate. Aphrodite was awarded the golden apple, and Paris got Helen, the most beautiful woman in the world.

There was one hitch to this prize—Helen was already married, to Menelaus, the king of Sparta. (Sparta was one of several small states in Greece, each ruled by its own king.) In spite of this, Paris journeyed to Sparta and was royally entertained by Menelaus and Queen Helen.

After some days of feasts and entertainment, Menelaus had to leave on a business trip to see the king of Knossos on the island of Crete near Greece. When Menelaus was gone, so says the legend, Paris eloped with Helen to Troy. Legends differ on whether Helen was a willing partner in the escape.

Homer tells us that Menelaus was still in Crete when he heard what had happened. Furious, he hastened back to Greece to enlist the help of his brother, King Agamemnon. Agamemnon was ruler of Mycenae, a city that was then the most powerful in all of Greece. Agamemnon sent messengers to Troy, demanding that Helen be returned to Sparta.

The messengers were refused, so Menelaus journeyed around Greece, asking the kings of the various states to join him in an armed attack on the city of Troy. Homer lists the kingdoms that sent armies—Mycenae, Sparta, Pylos, Knossos, and others. There were 164 places that sent troops and ships to Troy. The leaders chose Agamemnon as the commander of the combined armies, since he was the mightiest king in Greece.

The Greeks sailed to the bay near Troy where they beached their ships and built a camp. Cities near Troy helped the Trojan army fight off the Greeks. For years the fighting continued, first one side having the upper hand, then the other. Most of the soldiers were

This painting from a Greek vase shows Paris leading his prize, Helen, by the hand. Some versions of the story say she went willingly with the handsome Paris; others say she was kidnapped.

on foot and used spears, swords, and shields, but Homer mentions quite a number of battles fought from horse-pulled chariots.

By the time the war was in its tenth year, many thousands of men had died. Still the Trojans refused to return Helen to the Greek army. They must have felt that to give her up would be the same as admitting defeat. The Trojan hero Hector fought Achilles, the bravest and most feared of the Greek warriors, outside the gates of Troy. Achilles was the victor in that fight, although he was killed soon after by Paris. At this point in the war the Greeks used the giant horse to enter the city walls and burned the city to the ground.

A Real War?

The question of whether or not there was a Trojan War was not an issue with the ancient Greeks. The poems were history. They were not legend; they were not myth. The Greeks thought of the poems as a sacred text, a history of the proud past that bound them

Hector and Ajax, two famous heroes of the Trojan war, battle. The "manes" on the soldiers' helmets are made of horsehair, a common adornment of the time.

together—in much the same way that the ancient Hebrews viewed the Bible. The *Iliad* and the *Odyssey* were reminders that their ancestors had been brave, honorable people who had walked and talked with the ancient gods.

Homer's tales were seen as evidence of that long-ago time. Herodotus, considered the "Father of History," wrote extensively in the fifth century B.C. about the Trojan War. The Greek philosopher Plato used Homer's poems to reconstruct early Greek history. Alexander the Great, who lived in the fourth century B.C., claimed that he was descended from the Greek hero Achilles. It was widely known that Alexander took a copy of the *Iliad* with him on every military campaign and slept with it under his pillow! On more than one occasion he made special trips to visit the site of Troy and prayed to the goddess Athena, who was said to watch over the city.

The ancient Romans, too, were confident that the tale of Troy was historical fact. They believed that there had been one Trojan warrior, called Aeneas, who

The Greeks believed that gods freely mingled with humans. Here, gods are descending to join the earthly battle.

had survived the massacre, and that he had gone on to found the city of Rome. Many Romans in ancient times thought of the site of Troy as a sacred reminder of their past. Julius Caesar, the emperor of Rome in the first century B.C., was said to have visited the little Greek settlement of Ilium built on the ruins of Troy, and to have wept at the ancient city's terrible destruction. There was even a time when Caesar seriously considered moving the empire's capital from Rome to Ilium.

As the ancient world passed away, there were new ideas about the so-called "sacred history" of the Greeks and Romans. The more "modern" historians of the fourth and fifth centuries A.D. no longer thought of the *Iliad* and the *Odyssey* as historically accurate. Christianity had become a powerful force in the world by the fourth century, and many Christian scholars were outraged at the kind of religion portrayed in Homer's poems. Homer's heroes lived in a world of more than one god. Indeed, the ancient Greeks believed strongly in scores of gods and goddesses. There were gods of war, of farming, of the sun, of childbirth, of hunting. There were hundreds of local gods and goddesses in every forest and river throughout the countryside.

Christian scholars were also upset by the important role that these gods and goddesses played in history. Homer's heroes not only believe in the gods—they often speak with them face-to-face. The god Poseidon's anger kept the Greek hero Odysseus from going directly home after the war, and the concern of the goddess Athena finally saved his life! This seemed blasphemous to the early Christians, as if there were not the proper distance between God and people.

There were other reasons, too, that these new scholars rejected the *Iliad* and the *Odyssey* as history. Geographically, Homer made no sense. Places he names and describes as gigantic, powerful cities sim-

"Many observers have denied that a country would fight a ten-year war over a runaway queen. These observers overlook the enormous pride of these old kings. They were perfectly capable of fighting a war over a woman."

Author I.G. Edmonds, *The Mysteries of Homer's Greeks*

"We suspect a war was fought over the (beautiful) Hellespont and not—as legend has it—the beautiful Helen."

Author Sam Elkin, *Search for a Lost City*

Opposite page: The Mediterranean area, where most of the great adventures of Homer's day took place.

ply did not exist. Mycenae, the seat of mighty Agamemnon's empire, the great city which supplied more than one hundred ships and thousands of men to the Greek army, had been no more than a small town throughout history. As for Troy, or Knossos, or the other places Homer mentions—either they were so small they could not be recognized, or there was no evidence that they had ever existed at all.

For such reasons, Homer's work became thought of as "sacrilegious." One sixth century A.D. historian called the *Iliad* and the *Odyssey* "the devil's entertainment." No longer was Homer considered a source of Greek history. It became fashionable to attack Homer as being totally without substance. His poetry was not, as it had once been, an authority for information about courage and honor in war. It was simply myth.

Yet while scholars and historians of the era could find reasons to question the sanctity of Homer, no one ever doubted that the *Iliad* and the *Odyssey* were poetic masterpieces—the finest literature in the Western

The blind poet Homer, carrying his poet's lyre, is led by his young guide.

world. Homer stood as the role model for great poetry; his art of language and style were without equal. Writers, poets, and playwrights through the ages, from Shakespeare in the Elizabethan age to twentieth century novelists, have referred to characters in the *Iliad* and the *Odyssey*.

Homer's work seemed to have found its place. For the next several centuries, the Trojan War was considered merely legend, but Homer's telling of the tales was established as a landmark in Western literature.

In the late nineteenth century, a middle-aged German without any scholarly background came on the scene. The man was Heinrich Schliemann, and he was convinced that there had indeed been a Trojan War. His goal, he said, was to prove it to the world.

Schliemann was the first of several people in the last century who changed the way the world looked at Homer. Because of Schliemann and those who came after him, we now have evidence that a Trojan War could very well have occurred. We have a new picture of "prehistoric" Greece and the kingdoms that flourished in that long-ago time. Schliemann and others have found evidence of a powerful Greek kingdom that was very capable of waging such a war as Homer describes.

Mysteries are often difficult to solve even when the trail is fresh. But the search for a prehistoric war, buried in thousands of years of dust and sand, with no records or witnesses, seems almost impossible. How did they do it? Where did they begin?

Heinrich Schliemann, the German businessman who was obsessed with solving the mystery of Troy.

This silhouette is based on an old Greek illustration of a ship powered by rowers. The figures at left are Helen and Paris running to the ship to escape from the kingdom of Menelaus.

Two

Who Could Solve
the Mystery of Troy?

The man who is credited with unearthing Troy in the late nineteenth century was not a scholar. He had no degree from a famous university. He had no formal training in ancient history or archaeology. He was, of all things, a very successful businessman. By the time Heinrich Schliemann was forty-six years old, he had amassed a fortune of more than eighteen million dollars!

In 1868 when Schliemann publicly announced his belief that Troy was a real city and that Homer's tale of the Trojan War was indeed historical fact, scholars weren't sure whether to laugh or to be outraged. Who was this man, this upstart? Where were his credentials? How dare he come crashing into their academic world with his crazy theories?

Schliemann not only announced his theories to the world; he also went on to prove many of them true. Some scholars criticized his methods; others called him brash and bold. Some questioned his motives, labeling him a fortune hunter. But by the time Heinrich Schliemann's lifework was complete, his findings had changed the study of world history. Even those who had criticized him at first later admitted that he had earned the title ''Father of Archaeology.''

Heinrich Schliemann's excavations turned up ruins of several different cities.
Here he is shown sketching his finds.

His passion for Troy began, he later wrote, when he was a boy of eight. His father had given him a book called *Universal History* for Christmas that year, and the book seemed to cast a spell over the boy. The pages were filled with stories and drawings of ancient tales, among them the Trojan War.

One page held young Heinrich's attention for a long time; on it was an engraving of the burning of Troy with its gigantic walls crumbling. Heinrich asked his father whether the author of the book had seen the city in person, because he was able to draw it so well.

"My son," he said, "that is merely illustration, a fancy of the artist's imagination."

But Heinrich pressed further. "Did Troy really have such walls, or was that fanciful, too?"

The hero Aeneas carries his father out of the burning city of Troy. This picture is said to have made such an impression on the young Heinrich Schliemann that it inspired his lifelong obsession with Troy.

His father hesitated, but then assured his son that the huge walls were probably real.

"Then," persisted the boy, "if such walls really existed, they cannot have been completely destroyed; they're just too big. There must be some pieces of them left."

Schliemann later recalled that he and his father sat together that day in 1880, talking about Troy and the high walls that surrounded it.

"I was determined," said Schliemann later, "that one day I would find the walls of that beautiful city. I knew that the Trojan War had happened in ancient days, but I was convinced that I could find some ruins, some trace of them remaining."

With this goal in mind, Heinrich approached his studies in school very seriously. He had a teacher who shared his passion for ancient history. He learned

The Trojan horse is pulled into the city. (From a medieval painting.)

Latin, one of the ancient languages, and discovered that the language was easy for him. When Heinrich was ten, he presented his father with a special gift that Christmas, an original essay written in Latin! It seemed for a time that the boy would follow a direct path from childhood to his dream—studying ancient history, perhaps attending one of the noted universities in Germany, and then embarking on a career as a finder of lost cities.

The Grocer's Apprentice

But the Schliemann family ran into serious financial problems while Heinrich was still young. His father could no longer afford to send him to the school where he was studying Latin and Greek. Instead, Heinrich was enrolled in a trade school where he would learn the practical skills of accounting and bookkeeping.

He did well at these subjects and at the age of fourteen was apprenticed to a grocer. The work was hard and the hours almost intolerable. Starting at five in the morning, Heinrich stocked shelves, waited on customers, swept out the store, and unloaded heavy barrels in the stockroom. His workday ended at 11:00 p.m.

Heinrich had no time for studying or reading. The tales of Greece and Troy seemed terribly far away. He found that what he had learned, especially in the area of ancient history, he was quickly forgetting. There simply was not time enough for Heinrich to work toward his dream. The boy grew more and more depressed.

Something happened in the grocer's, however, that rekindled the dream. A very drunk young man stumbled into the shop one day. In his drunken state he was loudly reciting something, some poetry perhaps. Though they were loud and slurred, with a lilting, singsong rhythm, the words nonetheless had a startling effect on young Heinrich. In his later years,

Homer. This sculpture was done long after Homer's death, so no one knows how much it actually resembles the great poet.

Schliemann vividly remembered asking the young man what he was reciting. "Homer," was the mumbled reply.

Heinrich was ecstatic. He had no idea at all what the words meant, yet he loved the melodic, rolling sounds. Homer! He must learn Homer; he must somehow break out of his poor existence so that he could learn these wonderful things.

A Man of Many Languages

The story of Heinrich Schliemann's rise from a poor grocer's apprentice would fill an entire book. It is a fascinating story of hard work, brilliance, and that elusive knack of being in the right place at the right time. For our purposes here, however, it seems sufficient to say that Schliemann left his job at the grocer's and began sharpening his bookkeeping and accounting skills at various jobs throughout Europe. He found, as did his employers, that he was an unbelievably quick learner. He worked for a time in a brokerage house, then for an international trading company. He finally struck off on his own as a buyer and seller of commodities such as cloth, dye, lumber, and even gold.

In all his business dealings, he was straightforward and self-confident, traits which would later serve him well as an archaeologist. He formed opinions and would act on them without delay. He was bold and aggressive, traits which his scholarly critics would later find annoying.

Schliemann had an uncanny ability to learn languages, and that ability enabled him to succeed rapidly in his business. Although he had had no formal language classes in school aside from a little Latin and Greek at the age of ten, he found that he was able to learn languages more easily than most people. His methods, however, were anything but traditional.

Schliemann did not bother with rules of grammar. His practice was to read the language aloud for several

"At the age of eight, having given the matter mature consideration, Heinrich Schliemann announced his intention to devote his life to the rediscovery of the lost city."

Author Will Durant, *The Life of Greece*

"The reader . . . needs to be wary of accepting the myth Schliemann put forward about himself. . . . We cannot, for instance, even be sure of the truth of his famous tale about his childhood."

Author Michael Wood, *In Search of the Trojan War*

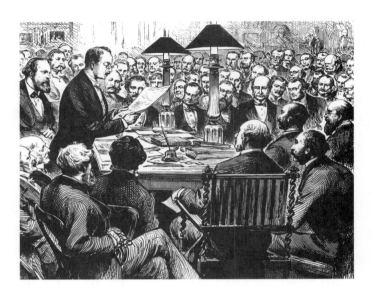

The distinguished and controversial Heinrich Schliemann lectures to a society of antiquarians (those who study ancient objects).

hours every day, even if he did not understand the meaning of the words. Then, he would compose little stories or essays in the new language and correct them with a teacher's help. He would memorize these stories and repeat them to himself, over and over. His memory was almost superhuman.

It was important for him to hear the language as often as possible, so he would seek out native speakers. This was not alway easy. When teaching himself English, for example, he found that the only way to hear it on a regular basis was to attend two masses each Sunday at a church with English-language services. By the time he was in his mid-thirties, Schliemann could speak and write fluently in a dozen languages.

This zeal for learning paid enormous economic dividends. Foreign businessmen visiting his firm were impressed and flattered that he spoke their language. They showed their appreciation by increasing the business they brought his way.

It is also interesting to learn that while he was adding languages to his repertoire, he purposely avoided learning ancient Greek, the language of Homer. Schliemann later recalled that he was a little afraid of the spell the language would cast over him. He had a feeling that should he throw himself into the study of Homer's poetry he might lose himself completely. Business, finances, even his personal life would surely suffer. Better, he thought, to wait until the right time for Homer and Troy.

Finally, at age forty-six, Schliemann the multimillionaire was restless. His marriage, never a happy one, had ended. All of his wheeling and dealing had paid off, but the challenge of business had lost its edge. He turned his sights toward Homer and Troy.

The Site of Bunarbashi

In the late nineteenth century most scholars believed that the war that Homer said raged for ten years around the city of Troy was a myth, that it had no

"From Calvert's letters we can be certain that at this time [August 1868] Schliemann espoused Lechevalier's Bunarbashi theory. . . . Hissarlik evidently had made no impression on him."

Author Michael Wood, *In Search of the Trojan War*

"One look from Heinrich Schliemann dismissed the mosquito-ridden village forever. Bunarbashi did not fit Homer's description of splendid Troy."

Author Sam Elkin, *Search for a Lost City*

This map is based on a very old map of the Troad, the area surrounding Troy.

factual basis. Although there were heaps of ruins from later settlements in the area of northwest Turkey where Troy was thought to be, no one seemed to be quite sure where Homer's ancient Troy might have stood. The general consensus, at least among the classical scholars in the universities of Europe, was that Troy was a poetic invention.

There was one school of thought, however, that said that Troy could have existed. First voiced by the French scholar Jean Baptiste Lechevalier, this theory maintained that if there had been a Troy, it must have been where the village of Bunarbashi now stands. Lechevalier had once walked the area in 1785 and found geographical similarities to Homer's descriptions of Troy. The most prominent similarity was a large spring which Lechevalier assumed could be Troy's hot and cold springs mentioned by Homer. Since Bunarbashi was certainly in the general area of what is now called the Trojan Plain, it seemed as logical a site as any for Troy.

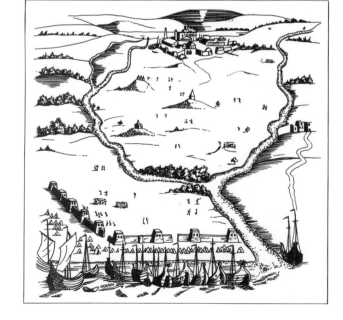

The great English poet, Alexander Pope, drew a rather fanciful map of Troy and the surrounding area, to illustrate his translation of Homer's *Iliad*. This drawing is based on Pope's map. The walls of the city are shown next to the water, with most of the buildings far in the background. Today, we know this is not accurate.

So those who believed that the mighty walls of Troy had once existed pointed to Bunarbashi. But no scholars in Schliemann's time had ever really done any digging or excavating. Archaeology as we know it today simply did not exist. True, a few ruins of ancient cities had been uncovered, but that was the work of treasure seekers rather than scientists or historians. Scholars' assertions were based on readings of ancient history.

It was to Bunarbashi, then, that Schliemann journeyed in the hot summer of 1868. He went alone, impeccably dressed as always and carrying a dog-eared copy of Homer in his coat pocket even though he had virtually memorized every line of the *Iliad* and the *Odyssey*.

Bunarbashi was a weary, filthy little Turkish village, quite a contrast to the beautiful city that some scholars claimed preceded it. It sat inland, about eight

An old carving in stone depicting the Trojan horse. Not many soldiers would have been able to hide in this version!

miles from the Aegean Sea. The distance from the sea bothered Schliemann. Homer stated that the Greeks had moved from their camp by the shore to the city walls sometimes as many as eight times a day. A three-hour march eight times a day? How could this be?

Schliemann had no trouble finding the famous springs of water. However, instead of two springs as Homer reported, there were more than forty! This, too, perplexed Schliemann. Wanting to be as careful and as thorough as possible, he tested the temperature of the springs with a pocket thermometer. All of the springs were the same temperature, 62.6 degrees Fahrenheit. So much, thought Schliemann, for the hot- and cold-spring idea, which had been the main argument for Bunarbashi as the site of Troy.

Standing in the steaming heat of Bunarbashi, referring once again to his copy of the *Iliad*, Schliemann read the Trojan hero Hector's cry to Achilles: "Three times I have fled around the mighty city of Priam, daring not to challenge you, but now, let me either slay or be slain."

With a crowd of curious Turkish peasants following him, Schliemann put the Bunarbashi site to the test. He tried running around the hill, as if he were

The hill at Hissarlik today. Signs of the excavations are evident on the top of the hill.

This late nineteenth-century etching shows the Hissarlik hill shortly after Schliemann's excavations were done. Some experts believe that the plain in the foreground was under water at one time.

Hector pursued by Achilles. When he got halfway around the hill, however, he had to stop. The south slope of the hill was a steep drop-off; he had to go down on all fours to keep his balance.

The crowd of villagers looked on in amazement as the little German millionaire in his fine suit carefully crept around the steep incline. "Only if Hector and Achilles had been mountain goats," he complained, "could this scene have happened at Bunarbashi."

Schliemann was almost positive that even though the surrounding countryside resembled the descriptions of Homer, Bunarbashi was not the right hill. However, just to be completely satisfied, he enlisted the help of some of the Turkish villagers. Armed with shovels and picks, they dug. Everywhere they dug, they struck rock within a few feet. There was nothing under Bunarbashi.

If Schliemann was right about the site of Bunarbashi, then where *was* the city of Troy? For

A diagram of the city of Troy, showing changes in different periods.

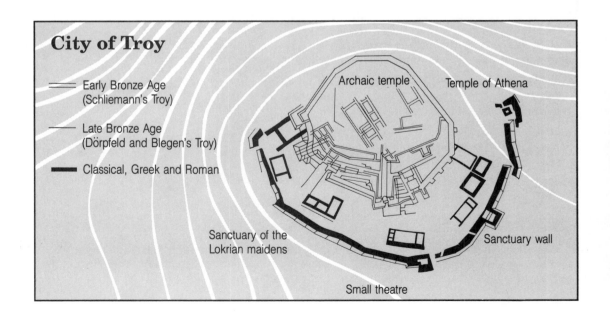

City of Troy

Early Bronze Age
(Schliemann's Troy)

Late Bronze Age
(Dörpfeld and Blegen's Troy)

Classical, Greek and Roman

Archaic temple

Temple of Athena

Sanctuary of the
Lokrian maidens

Sanctuary wall

Small theatre

days, he and his carriage driver rode around the area. Schliemann scanned every horizon, every view, searching for a place that looked right. Down every dusty, bumpy road they went, and even over territory that had no roads. Nothing resembled the area described by Homer.

A few months later he was contacted by a man named Frank Calvert, who had heard about Schliemann's interest in the area. Calvert and his brother owned part of a hill near the tiny village of Hissarlik, about three miles from the Aegean coast. Calvert was a British consul in the area and was himself interested in archaeology. He had done a little digging in part of the hill at Hissarlik and was convinced that ancient ruins of some sort lay within it. However, he had neither the time nor the money required to finance a large-scale project. Would Schliemann be interested in digging at Hissarlik?

Scholarly Evidence About Hissarlik

There was at least some scholarly support for Hissarlik as a possible site of Troy. Calvert knew of a Scottish geographer named Charles Maclaren who, although he had never visited Hissarlik, was able to piece together detailed maps of the area with ancient accounts by Greek and Roman writers. Though his theory received almost no support from scholarly circles, Maclaren felt that Hissarlik matched Homer's Troy quite well. Schliemann eagerly wrote back, telling Calvert that he would come to Hissarlik at once.

At Hissarlik Schliemann saw what he was looking for. Empty and desolate, the hill seemed to be consistent with Homer's descriptions. It was completely uninhabited except for an occasional grazing goat. The hot summer winds blew in swirls. As Calvert had mentioned, the hill was only three miles from the sea; the Greeks could easily have made many trips back and forth from their camp to this site. Taking out his stopwatch, Schliemann gave the hill the "three times

"After carefully examining the Trojan plain on two occasions, I fully agree with the conviction of this savant [Calvert] that the high plateau of Hissarlik is the position of ancient Troy."

Heinrich Schliemann, quoted in *In Search of Ancient Troy*

"In fact Schliemann entirely owed this idea to Calvert. . . . Schliemann had only the dimmest recollection of what Hissarlik had actually *looked like*!"

Author Michael Wood, *In Search of the Trojan War*

The sea is faintly visible in the background of this photograph taken from Hissarlik hill. The Trojans were at least this close to the sea, and perhaps closer, since the water probably covered more of the Trojan plain than it does today.

around'' test, and it passed! Certainly, Hector and Achilles could have circled this hill in the rage of battle with no problem.

He later wrote in his journal that he ''intuitively knew'' that Hissarlik was the site of ancient Troy. He needed no further proof—his instincts told him that he was right. But Schliemann's instincts would not convince the historians and scholars of the late nineteenth century. He needed concrete proof. Perhaps he could find traces of those ancient walls or unearth a helmet worn by one of the soldiers who fought in the Trojan War. In his diary Schliemann fantasized finding the spear and armor of the great Achilles himself. What a treasure that would be!

All he needed to do, he decided, was to get permission to dig under the hill, and then he could begin. And in that bold, brash style that helped him earn millions in the world of business, that is just what he set out to do.

A golden bottle from the great treasure.

Three

Was Troy at Hissarlik?

In early autumn of 1871 Heinrich Schliemann arrived at Hissarlik, ready to dig. He was newly remarried; his young Greek wife, Sophie, accompanied him. As usual, he carried his worn copy of the *Iliad*. He was very confident that Troy lay under the hill at Hissarlik, just waiting to be discovered.

It had taken more than a year for Schliemann to obtain permission from the Turkish government to carry on any excavations. The Turks were instantly suspicious of this bold little businessman from Germany. Why would he be interested in digging up a remote hill in their country, they asked? Was he a spy, interested perhaps in the fortifications the government had built nearby? Or was there some valuable treasure beneath the surface? If so, it should belong to Turkey, not to this millionaire in his impeccably-tailored suit.

After a great deal of discussion on both sides, and with Frank Calvert pulling some strings on Schliemann's behalf, the Turks finally agreed that Schliemann could dig. However, they insisted that there be a representative from the Turkish government on the site at all times.

Schliemann hired men from nearby villages to help him dig. He paid each worker nine *piasters* (approximately twenty-two cents) per day. The men used picks and heavy shovels, and carried away the dirt and debris in large straw baskets. Schliemann was everywhere,

Schliemann's Hissarlik dig in progress. Rubble was transported and dumped over the edge of the hill with the rail car.

calling out to his workers to hurry, to dig deeper and faster. He felt that finding the city of Troy before the raw winter winds and cold rains set in was important.

Layers of Walls

Almost within an hour of digging, Schliemann discovered ancient walls. He was convinced that they were the walls of Troy, the city of King Priam. Ecstatic, he crowed, ''I have found Priam's city! Troy lives!''

His jubilation was short-lived, however. His workers found that the walls had been built over other walls. These first walls were modern compared with Homer's Troy: They probably dated from the first century after Christ. Occasionally the workers dug up copper coins, and by dating these, Schliemann substantiated the age of the first walls. It was becoming clear to Schliemann that they would have to dig much deeper.

It had never dawned on Schliemann that there would be more than one city under this hill. But he

Worker at Hissarlik sitting in the midst of walls from various periods.

A Turkish worker stands near the great trench Schliemann cut through the Trojan site.

assumed, mostly based on Homer's tale, that Troy was the original city on the site. If that were true, then Troy would be the bottom layer. The layers on top needed to be cleared away, he reasoned, so that Troy could be seen.

Irreparable Mistakes

Based on this theory, Schliemann devised a new strategy for digging Hissarlik. He would simply remove whatever was not pertinent to ancient Troy and dump it over the side of the hill.

Back through time Schliemann and his work force traveled, through layer after layer of cities. It became apparent that these ancient people never really bothered to clear away debris from a ruined city or village. They simply whisked away the surface rubbish, flattened out the area, and built their own new village! As the work progressed, Schliemann found that he was able to venture educated guesses as to the reason one level or layer ended and a new one began. In several areas the stones were blackened, most likely

Above: "Schliemann's Folly," the great trench Schliemann carelessly dug in his eagerness to reach "the real Troy." He found out later that he had destroyed much valuable evidence about Troy and the other cities that had been on the same site.
Below: Even a small fragment of pottery, such as this one from Troy I, the bottommost layer at Hissarlik, can give scholars important clues to the life and culture of those who made it. Unfortunately, Schliemann hadn't known how significant such "trash" could be.

by fire. Some layers were totally scrambled, as though an earthquake had upheaved them. Some layers might have been destroyed by wars.

Unfortunately, Schliemann had no time for anything that did not relate to Homer's Troy. These other cities might be interesting to some scholars sitting in armchairs in the universities of Europe, but Schliemann's was a single-minded task.

"Schliemann's Folly"

By the time winter hit the hill at Hissarlik, Schliemann knew that he had to come up with a better way of digging. Peeling away each city layer by layer was time-consuming. He decided that he would dig an enormous ditch, a long trench through the hill. The ditch would stretch more than four hundred feet long, and would be almost one hundred feet wide. By exposing the hillside in this way, Schliemann decided, he could get to what he called "virgin soil." When he came to that point, he would know that he had reached the original city of Troy. He noted at the time that destroying so much of the hill would be unfortunate, but such was the price of discovery.

This bold, assertive style was essential to Schliemann the businessman, but it proved regrettable for Schliemann the archaeologist. In his haste to unearth Troy, he destroyed whatever lay in his path. Cities, ancient homes, temples to the long-ago gods and goddesses—most were destroyed by the picks and shovels and were unceremoniously dumped over the hill in pieces. Fragments of pottery were completely destroyed. Archaeologists now know that pottery can give priceless clues about the ancient people who fashioned and used it. All of these were important links with the past, and none can ever be accurately recovered.

It is easy from our vantage point to criticize Schliemann for being so obsessed with Troy that he destroyed everything else. But it is important to remember that the science of archaeology was non-existent in Schliemann's time. No one had attempted to do what he was doing. There were no textbooks or manuals to explain how to preserve the irrelevant material while bringing to light that which was relevant. Schliemann had to rely on trial and error, but he *did* learn as he went on. Gradually he realized that it would be helpful to keep careful records of the objects he found. He began documenting his finds, describing them in detail, and, more important, noting the depth at which he recovered each item. That would later help him sort through the hundreds of thousands of objects he was accumulating.

Virgin Soil and a Disappointment

When at last Schliemann hit virgin soil, he was horrified. He had been certain that when he came to the final level, he would find Troy. But the original city, the one at the bottom of this nest of cities under the hill at Hissarlik, was far earlier than the Troy of Homer.

This was a Stone Age settlement. It lay fifty-three feet from the surface of the hill. Schliemann uncovered many houses crudely built of stones that were loosely joined with mud. He found many examples of pottery and cups as well as an assortment of stone tools. At the time, Schliemann had no way of accurately dating the settlement, but modern archaeologists estimate that the village dates between 3000-2500 B.C., more than a thousand years before the Trojan War could have taken place!

"Schliemann decided to drive vast trenches through the mound, removing hundreds of tons of earth and rubble, demolishing earlier structures which stood in his way. . . . What is left is the ruin of a ruin."

Author Michael Wood, *In Search of the Trojan War*

"Some archaeologists condemn Schliemann for his ruthless destruction of ancient artifacts. But is this not like condemning a man for not learning to steer the cart before the invention of the wheel?"

Author Sam Elkin, *Search for a Lost City*

This dagger from Troy I is made from an ox rib. The simplicity of the material and the finished blade tell scientists that the Troy I culture was much more primitive than later cultures on the same site.

Troy I wall and tower.

The people who inhabited the village were primitive in that they used only stone for tools and weapons; they had not yet learned to use bronze or iron. This could not be the Troy of Homer because the inhabitants of that city had swords and shields fashioned from bronze and gold. So, if this settlement was not Troy, and it obviously was not, that meant to Schliemann that Troy was not the original city on the hill. He had dug right through it—undoubtedly destroying part of it as he had destroyed parts of the other cities.

He turned back to the other cities that were exposed in layers on the hill. Which was Troy? There were, he was sure, six different cities under Hissarlik. It was difficult to keep the settlements clear in his own mind, however, for they were not flat and even like layers of a cake. When building a settlement these ancient people did not start with an even plain. One family's house may have been built on higher ground than another family's house, higher perhaps because whatever was underneath it from an earlier settlement was higher. This made the layers, or *strata*, of the cities under Hissarlik blend together in puzzling ways. Schliemann was frustrated and confused.

It became Schliemann's self-appointed task, then, to sift through the six layers to find the true Troy. He took on additional crew members, and cautioned them

Walls from different time periods in Troy's history. Notice the different shapes of the stones and the different levels of sophistication in the ways the stones are put together.

to be extremely careful with each spadeful of dirt. Since Troy could be anywhere in the hill, he didn't want to repeat his earlier mistake.

The seventh city, lying closest to the surface of Hissarlik, was clearly not Troy. Only six feet underground, this settlement was full of marble columns, mosaic floors, and sculptures—all indicating that the city was inhabited by Greeks of Homer's day. This city was built during the period of "classical" Greece.

The sixth city was the most puzzling to Schliemann. Among its ruins he found a great deal of a strange kind of gray pottery—unlike anything he had seen in the other strata. The abrupt change in pottery style seemed to indicate that the settlement was inhabited—quite possibly taken over—by a foreign people. These people had brought with them their methods of making pottery, which differed completely from the style of the former inhabitants. Who these new people were was a mystery.

"This city [Troy II] answers perfectly to the Homeric description of the site of sacred Ilios. . . . My work at Troy is now ended forever."

Heinrich Schliemann, 1882, quoted in *In Search of the Trojan War*

"Troy II, the city Schliemann thought was Ilium, was built around 2500 BC. The Troy of Achilles, Priam, Paris, Hector, Odysseus, and the eternally lovely Helen is now believed to have been Troy VII-a."

Author I.G. Edmonds, *The Mysteries of Troy*

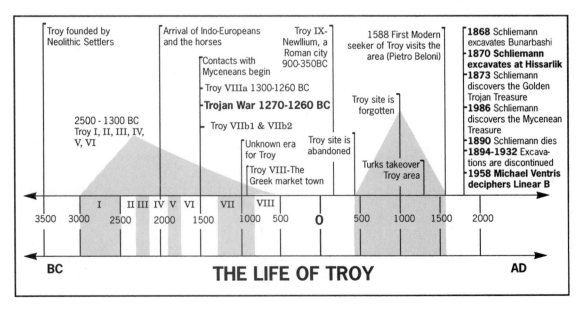

THE LIFE OF TROY

Cyclopean walls at Mycenae, another city that is important to the history of the Trojan war. The gateway in the background is much taller than the height of a person. This helps show how huge the stones are. Perhaps you can see why it was thought that only a giant, like the Cyclops, would be capable of building a wall with such stones.

The fifth and fourth settlements had houses made of wood and clay. This style of building seemed much too primitive to be considered seriously. The third city interested Schliemann at first because it had been razed by fire. Could this have been Troy, set on fire by the attacking Greek army? But this third settlement had none of the grand walls, watchtowers, and gates associated with Homer's Troy. This city, like the fourth and fifth cities above it, was mostly built of wood and clay. Schliemann dismissed it.

The second settlement of Hissarlik seemed more promising to Schliemann. Located forty-five feet below the surface, this city had brick houses built by a more advanced method than the houses of the first layer. This second city, like the third one, apparently had been destroyed by a great fire. The bricks which were not burned had turned a dark red and each of the stones recovered from that layer was blackened by the intense heat. Images of the burning walls of Homer's Troy must have excited Schliemann. Could this be the city?

An Extraordinary Find

Again his bold, brash confidence appeared. Yes, this was definitely Troy. He busied himself writing press releases to European newspapers. He had found Troy, and more evidence would be forthcoming.

The evidence continued to mount. Workers found melted copper and lead throughout the layer, further indicating that this city had been destroyed by intense heat. The base of a tall stone lookout tower was uncovered. Massive walls, called *Cyclopean walls* (because it was once thought that only a huge Cyclops could build them), were found in this second settlement. Were these the walls through which the unknowing Trojans pulled the famous wooden horse? Schliemann rejoiced, and he was quick to boast, ''I have found the walls of Troy! I have found the palace walls of King Priam!''

In late May 1873, just a few days before Schliemann and his wife were to close the digging site and move on, an extraordinary find was made. As the crews were beginning the day's work, Schliemann caught sight of something glinting in the dirt. He quietly called Sophie's attention to the sparkling object and told her to give the men a rest period.

When Sophie hesitated, worrying that the men would become suspicious of a rest so soon after the start of the day, Schliemann thought of another plan. "Tell the men that today is my birthday," he suggested. "Tell them that I am taking the day off, and they should, too."

Sophie shouted, "*Paidos*, stop working," to the men. Delighted, they trooped home. As soon as Schliemann and Sophie were alone, he took out a knife and loosened the object from the earth. It was a copper container about twelve inches long. As he removed the bowl, he could see gold behind it—more gold than he had ever seen in one place.

Motioning for Sophie to come to his side, he filled her shawl with objects. She walked casually to their quarters and returned to fill up her shawl again. After several trips, trying to suppress their excitement, Schliemann and his wife locked themselves in their small living quarters and gazed at what they had unearthed.

A Golden Treasure

It was a treasure beyond anything he had ever hoped to find. In all, there were 8,700 pieces, ranging from bars of solid silver to bronze battle-axes. And there was gold: goblets, necklaces, earrings, buttons, and rings. One ornate crown, called a diadem, contained over 2,000 pure gold chain links, charms, leaves, and rings! A necklace contained more than 4,000 separate pieces of gold.

Again Schliemann was aggressive in his proclamations. As far as he was concerned, he had found the

"Priam's treasure." A portion of the great treasures Schliemann found at Hissarlik.

"Since I found all the objects together . . . it seems certain that they lay in a wooden chest, of the kind mentioned in the *Iliad* as having been in Priam's Palace."

Heinrich Schliemann, quoted in *The Bull of Minos*

"He believed that the golden treasure he found had belonged to King Priam. He was wrong."

Author Sam Elkin, *Search for a Lost City*

treasure of Priam, the jewels of Helen. In his mind, there was no doubt that this second city was the Troy of which Homer spoke. Calling it Troy II (he had decided to refer to each of the seven layers by number, the oldest at the bottom being Troy I, and so on) he announced in press releases from Hissarlik that he was certain that Homer's Troy had been found.

Skeptical Scholars

The reaction of scholars and historians to Schliemann's announcement was mostly negative. Some, like Professor R.C. Jebb of Scotland and classical scholar Rudolf Stephani of Russia, were critical of Schliemann's claim that he had found King Priam's treasure. How could he be so sure the treasure was Priam's? There were no inscriptions on any of the pieces that would prove ownership. Historian E. Brentano of Frankfurt was suspicious of Schliemann's knowledge of dating artifacts and called Schliemann's claims "brittle and rotten."

Many scholars agreed with Brentano. They found absurd the very idea of someone like Schliemann, an academic nobody, making such discoveries. True scholarship was accomplished by real scholars, they

Workers cart rubbish and seek treasure at Hissarlik.

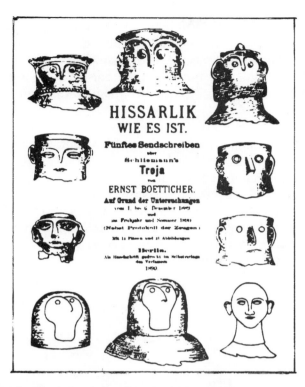

Title page from a pamphlet by Ernst Bötticher, one of Schliemann's critics. Bötticher believed that Schliemann had found only an old burial site, not the ancient city of Troy.

maintained. A businessman and his wife, without university degrees, did not qualify as historians of ancient Greece, no matter what they dug out of the ground.

A few of Schliemann's critics even accused him of faking the whole thing. The director of the Athens University Library said publicly that Schliemann had discovered his treasure "not at Hissarlik but at the second-hand dealers." In reaction to this remark, Schliemann summoned an official of the British Museum, who examined the artifacts carefully. The official announced soon afterward that the treasure find was authentic, although he could not date it specifically.

There were some authorities on ancient Greece who defended Schliemann, although they too felt he was impulsive in his conclusions. One of these, Pro-

Sophie Schliemann,
Heinrich's Greek wife,
wearing a gold diadem from
the treasure of Troy.

fessor Rudolf Virchow of Berlin, congratulated Schliemann on spending so much time and money on the Hissarlik project. "The Burnt City would still have lain to this day hidden in the earth," Virchow publicly declared, "had not imagination guided the spade."

The reaction of the Turkish government to Schliemann's find was very clear-cut; they wanted Schliemann to hand the treasure over to them. Schliemann had no intention of letting the Turkish authorities keep the treasure, however, and secretly moved it to Europe. The treasure was never sold, but most of it mysteriously disappeared in Berlin in 1945. The few pieces which did survive are on display at the Istanbul Museum.

This German cartoon makes fun of Schliemann's eagerness to find treasure. The *Nibelungen* is a German saga which tells of a wondrous treasure called the Rhine gold. The cartoon suggests that greedy Sophie and Heinrich are setting out after this fabled gold too.

Feeling confident that he had brought the ancient city of Troy to light for all the world, Schliemann wanted to turn his sights to other cities mentioned by Homer. The discovery at Troy created more questions in Schliemann's mind, and he wanted to answer them.

That there had been a Troy was no proof that there had been a war. Who had set the walls of Troy on fire? Could there actually have been ancient Greeks in prehistoric times capable of mounting such an attack on a foreign power as strong as Troy?

Below: Key to wooden box holding Trojan treasure.

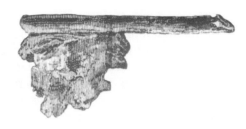

Four

What Was the Connection with Mycenae?

By locating the ancient city of Troy, Schliemann opened the door for a closer look at Homer. For centuries Homer had been considered a great poet, but few believed that his poems were based on real events. With the discoveries at Hissarlik, Schliemann felt he had made a good start in his quest for the historical Trojan War. That there was indeed a mighty city in the location Homer described, however, was not nearly enough to prove Homer's accuracy. So, Schliemann turned his sights from the Trojans to their enemies in war, the prehistoric Greeks.

The Greeks of the *Iliad* and the *Odyssey* lived in small kingdoms: Tiryns, Pylos, and Ithaca, to name a few. These kingdoms were joined in a sort of confederation, with Agamemnon, the ruler of the kingdom of Mycenae, as their overlord. Homer called the city of Mycenae "rich in gold" and Agamemnon "the king of men." As overlord of the Greek kingdoms Agamemnon also served as the commander of the entire Greek army. Homer says that Agamemnon contributed no fewer than one hundred ships to the military campaign against Troy. He led the Greeks to victory over the Trojans and afterward sailed home to Mycenae. In the *Odyssey* we learn that upon his return Agamemnon was brutally murdered by his wife, Clytemnestra, and a rival to his throne.

Fabulous gold mask found by Schliemann at Mycenae. He believed it was the funeral mask of Agamemnon.

Schliemann knew that in order to judge the accuracy of Homer's work, it was important to prove that Mycenae was really a center of power for these ancient Greeks. The task would be a hard one; in the eighth century B.C. when Homer composed his great epics, Mycenae was no more than a small town. Greece was not a well-organized collection of kingdoms. Instead, it was a smattering of disorganized petty states. The level of civilization in Homer's day was *far lower* than the prehistoric events he describes! Buildings were mud brick and wood, not cut stone as in the *Iliad*. Eighth century B.C. rulers did not live in lavish palaces, as did Agamemnon. Precious materials such as gold and ivory were extremely rare in Homer's day—yet the poet goes into great detail about the gold, silver, and jewels possessed by the Greeks five hundred years earlier.

The ancient Greek world. Troy is slightly above and to the right of the word *Aegean*; Mycenae is to the left of the same word.

If he could somehow prove that Mycenae had been a city of great importance, if he could show that the Greeks had actually been more powerful five centuries before Homer, Schliemann felt certain that Homer's poems could be considered valid history. The task seemed immense, but Schliemann plunged into it with his usual headstrong enthusiasm. For Schliemann and his successors, however, Mycenae presented at least one less problem than Troy had. Unlike Troy, Mycenae had not vanished underground. The site had never been in doubt; its Cyclopean walls and impressive Lion Gate were visible reminders that the city was ancient. But where was the evidence of a mighty civilization? Where was Mycenae ''rich in gold''?

Following Directions

Others had explored the site before Schliemann, and had found impressive ruins outside the main fortress, or *citadel*. Decorative marble friezes [a band of decoration around the top of a wall] in red and black and the Lion Gate were hailed by some early excavators as ''without equal anywhere.'' Among those early explorers were William Leake and William Gell. Both had visited Mycenae in the early part of the nineteenth century. Leake, a historical geographer, con-

The famous Lion Gate, an entrance to the city of Mycenae.

Ruins of the imposing citadel of Mycenae.

This map shows roughly the way the city of Mycenae was laid out. The heavy dark outline represents the city's walls. The grave circle on the left is where Schliemann found his great Mycenaean treasure.

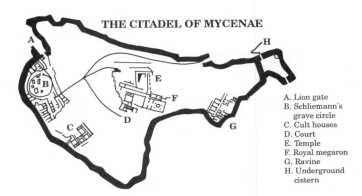

THE CITADEL OF MYCENAE

A. Lion gate
B. Schliemann's grave circle
C. Cult houses
D. Court
E. Temple
F. Royal megaron
G. Ravine
H. Underground cistern

"We now know for certain that there was a siege and sack of Troy near the end of the Mycenaean period; and we know that . . . in the area concerned, Greek military and commercial forces were at work."

Denys Page, Cambridge University Professor of Greek, *The Greek World*

"Hissarlik was twice destroyed in the Helladic epoch, once by earthquake and once by Thracians; but no evidence has been found for any destruction at the hands of Greek mainlanders."

Rhys Carpenter, Professor Emeritus of Classical Archaeology at Bryn Mawr College, *Folk Tale, Fiction and Saga in the Homeric Epics*

structed an excellent description and detailed map of the area. Gell, a noted British historian, searched for bits of fragmented sculpture which he tried to catalogue.

Some of Schliemann's predecessors had been simply treasure hunters, looking for gold in tombs that were thought to be outside the city wall. When Schliemann arrived at Mycenae in the summer of 1876, however, he was certain that any tombs containing royalty and their gold would be *within* the walls. His source was a Greek traveler named Pausanias, who had lived in the second century A.D. Pausanias had written a journal of his travels called *Guidebook to Greece*. He wrote that when he had visited Mycenae he was shown graves of Agamemnon and several of his companions. Pausanias claimed these graves were within the walls.

With this ancient journal in mind, Schliemann began digging just inside the Lion Gate. He was aware of the losses he had caused at Hissarlik with his impatience, so he was very careful not to damage anything his work crew uncovered. Slowly, painstakingly, Schliemann and his men dug to ten feet, then deeper into the earth.

There he found upright stone markers indicating the presence of five grave shafts. Many of the markers

Above: An old etching of the grave circle at Mycenae. The holes in the ground are the excavated graves where Schliemann found ancient bodies "smothered in gold." Left: A modern photograph of the same site.

A portion of one of the decorated grave slabs.

were ornately decorated with scenes of battle and hunting. Digging down into the first of the five shafts, he came upon three bodies literally covered in gold. These people were, Schliemann wrote, ''smothered in gold''—gold rings, diadems, breastplates, and weapons. A few of the bones and skulls had partially survived but they crumbled when the tombs were opened and exposed to the moisture of the air.

Quickly Schliemann ordered the other graves excavated. More bodies were found, each more lavishly decorated than the last. In all, the remains of nineteen men and women and two infants were uncovered. There were gold and silver goblets and hundreds of gold circular disks which were, by any civilization's standards, artistic masterpieces.

Some bodies were decorated with hundreds of gold plates in the shape of shields. Some were layered with jewels. Four of the men's bodies wore death masks of solid gold, and one of these, Schliemann insisted, was the mask of Agamemnon. It was a mask resembling the face of a lion, and Schliemann was aware that the lion has often been used as a symbol of royalty. So sure was Schliemann that this mask not only belonged to a king, but that the king was Agamemnon, that he reportedly wept and sent a telegram to the King of Greece announcing, ''I have gazed upon the face of Agamemnon!''

A small selection from the incredible golden treasure Schliemann found at Mycenae.

Schliemann achieved worldwide fame for this find that was more spectacular even than his find at Hissarlik. The treasure of Mycenae was turned over to the Greek government and has been on display in Athens since. For the most part, Schliemann's critics were silenced, although there were a few who questioned his assumption that the graves belonged to Agamemnon's dynasty. Many of the noted scholars in Europe's universities were supportive. Max Müller of Oxford University in England wrote to Schliemann, congratulating him on an exciting discovery and telling him to ignore the critics. "Never mind the attacks of the press. . . . They are soon forgotten, even if they are read," Müller wrote. British Prime Minister William Gladstone was wholeheartedly behind Schliemann and offered to write the preface to Schliemann's book about the Mycenaean excavation.

Schliemann dug at a few more sites in Greece, all of them cities mentioned by Homer. He was certain that the more prehistoric ruins he could unearth, the more chances he would have to bring the Trojan

Curious museum visitors examine some of Schliemann's finds, on display in Athens.

War to light. He even returned to Hissarlik, hoping to find a connection between Troy II and Mycenae; but he found nothing that would indicate interaction between the two great cities. He died in 1890.

Continuing the Search

Despite her husband's death, Sophie Schliemann wanted to continue the work at Hissarlik, and in 1893 she sponsored an excavation under the direction of Wilhelm Dörpfeld. Dörpfeld was a specialist in ancient architecture and he had a brilliant knack for noticing detail that otherwise might go unrecognized. He had served Schliemann as a consultant at some of the later excavations. In fact, Schliemann had relied on him often at Hissarlik for making sense of the architectural styles evident in the various layers.

In two years of excavating, from 1893 to 1894, Dörpfeld made some exciting discoveries. Digging at the southern slope of Hissarlik, he uncovered massive city walls, over three hundred feet of them in all. The walls were beautifully crafted out of cut limestone. He found watchtowers, too, which stood twenty-five feet high. There were two gates, one on the east end, and the other on the south. This was Schliemann's sixth level; evidently the walls had seemed to him too well made or modern looking to be Homer's Troy, so he had dug right through them!

Heinrich Schliemann poses with colleagues at Hissarlik. Schliemann is seated at front.

Dörpfeld found five houses within these city walls. The houses were spacious and airy, and, Dörpfeld thought, "architecturally brilliant." This city had been destroyed by fire, just as Schliemann's Troy II had been. Dörpfeld was beginning to believe that he had found the real level of Troy. To add to the mounting evidence, many Mycenaean pottery fragments (perhaps from the invading Greek army?) were found in this sixth layer. Scholars were becoming more interested by the minute.

Since pottery styles are simple identifying marks of any ancient civilization, the finding of pots—even broken pieces, called *potsherds*—are important to archaeologists. Every tribe or civilization had its own way of making cups, storage jars, and bowls. The style may be reflected in the type of clay or the technique of "firing" the pots. It may be evident in the colors and symbols painted on the pottery.

When people change the way they make pottery, they do so gradually. Even though they may find a new style or shape, there are things about the new pots that stay the same; there is always some link with the old style. If a completely new pottery type is found in ancient ruins, archaeologists assume that either the settlement was taken over by a new group of people with different pottery, or that the settlement entered into a trading relationship with a foreign people.

The Mycenaean pottery that Dörpfeld found in the sixth layer was just the link that Schliemann had been searching for prior to his death. And now in 1894, four years after his death, the search for Troy appeared to be over.

The Cincinnati Expedition

In the forty years following Schliemann's announcement that he had found Homer's Troy at Hissarlik, archaeology made great advances. Methods of dating pottery and other artifacts became more exact. Not only had it become easier to pinpoint the age

A fragment of telltale pottery. This piece shows warriors marching off to battle.

of ruins, there were more sophisticated ways of retrieving layers of those ruins from the ground.

Carl Blegen was an American archaeologist who had not even been born when Schliemann was making his most exciting discoveries. Like Schliemann before him, Blegen strongly believed that there was truth behind Homer's tales. So, in 1932 Blegen led a team of archaeologists from the University of Cincinnati to dig further at Hissarlik.

By working with more modern methods, Blegen was able to identify nine distinct layers of cities at the site—three more than Schliemann had found. Some of these layers had layers *within* layers, which means that settlements which were destroyed or conquered were immediately rebuilt and inhabited. There was no rubble or debris separating these small layers.

Schliemann's Troy II, the one he thought was Homer's Troy and that layer at which he found the "Treasure of Priam," was now dated at about 2500 B.C., roughly one thousand years before the Trojan War could have happened.

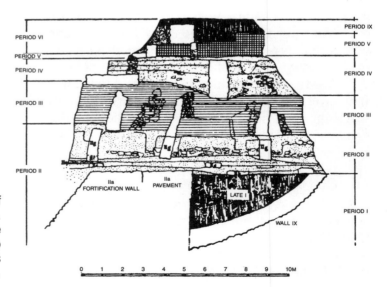

A view of the nine layers of cities found at the Troy site. Drawn by Carl Blegen, one of the scientists who improved upon Schliemann's findings.

Upon examining the sixth layer, where in 1894 Wilhelm Dörpfeld had uncovered what he thought was Homer's Troy, Blegen noticed that many of the walls had actually shifted at their foundations. Some of the walls had crumbled and toppled over. This, surely, was not the work of Agamemnon's army. Further tests indicated, and Dörpfeld himself agreed, that this city had been destroyed by an earthquake. The potsherds still proved that this beautiful city had had commerce of some kind with the ancient Mycenaeans, but this Troy, dating between 1500 and 1300 B.C., was not Priam's citadel.

Blegen reckoned that the site at layer six had been immediately reinhabited after the earthquake. The new site, which he labeled Troy VII A, was rebuilt by the

Top: A modern photograph shows the "potholes," the strange holes that were discovered in the excavations. They were discovered to be the locations of buried jars used to store oil and other foodstuffs. Below: an old etching showing the jars, many of them six feet tall.

"The presence of Mycenaean pottery convinced Dörpfeld that Schliemann had been wrong and that Troy VI, not Troy II, had been destroyed by the vengeful Greek."

Author I.G. Edmonds, *The Mysteries of Troy*

"Blegen became convinced that the destruction of Troy VI could not have been by the hand of man, as Dörpfeld had thought. . . . Troy VI, the city of the great walls, had been destroyed by an earthquake, not by Agamemnon's army."

Author Michael Wood, *In Search of the Trojan War*

same people. For the most part the walls still stood, but sections were damaged. Streets that had once been wide and open were now filled with hastily-built shacks bunched together. Large storage pots for holding oil and grain were sunk into the floors of these shacks. Evidence indicated that people of this settlement were frightened about something and had crowded together for protection.

Blegen put forth the theory that the city was sheltering a much larger population than it could reasonably hold. Perhaps those living in the areas outside the city walls had to come inside for protection—from Agamemnon's warriors? It is almost impossible to say for sure. This city did perish in a great fire, however, so that much coincides with Homer's tale. The dating of this settlement was set at about 1300 B.C., with the fire occurring at about 1260 B.C. This is definitely within what was thought to be the appropriate time frame for the Trojan War.

Carl Blegen found evidence that Troy VI was destroyed by earthquake.

What Blegen found stands today as the final chapter on the site of ancient Troy; his findings were then, and are now, accepted by the academic world as valid. The response to Blegen's work was, as historian Michael Wood describes it, ''a grateful, even joyful one among the majority of classical scholars.'' Here, finally, was proof that the city of Troy not only existed, but was sacked, just as Homer reported.

The Contribution of Schliemann

Schliemann was wrong about the second level of Hissarlik. He also, as was shown later, was wrong about the gold at Mycenae. Because of the use of modern chemical dating techniques we now know that the treasure he uncovered there was from the sixteenth-century B.C., three hundred years before Agamemnon's time.

Yet the most important contribution of Heinrich Schliemann was not his ability to interpret that which he uncovered. Rather, it was his discovery that the eighth-century poems of Homer are almost certainly based on truth—that is the valuable contribution for which Schliemann will be remembered. Schliemann's work opened up a vast, uncharted territory for those who study ancient history.

Heinrich Schliemann, the first modern person to find proof that Homer's great epics were more than myth.

Five

Who Were the Mycenaeans?

In his excavations at Mycenae, Tiryns, and other cities on the Greek mainland, Schliemann uncovered hundreds of thousands of artifacts. Many of these items seem to be evidence of a rich and exciting heroic age in prehistory, an age when an ancient people based on mainland Greece seemed to be very powerful. Schliemann called these people *Mycenaeans* because the city of Mycenae was one of their most important citadels. If Homer was reporting real history, it was quite likely these Mycenaeans, the prehistoric Greeks of the *Iliad*, who attacked and destroyed Troy. But there were many unanswered questions about this ancient people. Who were these people led by Agamemnon? How do we know the extent of their power in the thirteenth century B.C., the legendary time of the Trojan War? Did it reach throughout the Greek mainland, as Homer claimed?

Palaces of Blood

The main citadel at Mycenae is a gloomy, imposing structure. The royal palace sprawls on a hill between two mountain peaks. There is a deep ravine on one side and steep slopes on the others. Clearly, this place was built with fortification in mind.

As this illustration shows, the interiors of palaces at the time of Troy and Mycenae were elaborately decorated. What is left today may be mostly bare rubble, but once these places were glorious.

The other citadels of mainland Greece are of the same mold. They were all fortified with walls of immense stone blocks—Cyclopean walls. The gates to the citadels are usually in a section of wall folded back in a narrow U-shape, so that an invading army trying to break in the gate could be bombarded with spears, rocks, and arrows by the citadel's warriors.

From studying the palaces at Pylos, Mycenae, and Tiryns, archaeologists have found that the king or chief lived in a large section of the palace called a *megaron*. In addition to the megaron, each palace had a great hall which contained a central hearth and plenty of storeroom space. There were even underground fountains within the walls with hidden staircases leading to them in case an enemy tried to cut off access to the city's water supply.

The Mycenaeans were, without a doubt, a warlike people; the archaeology of their palaces and citadels is proof. Schliemann and his successors revealed a civilization of constant warfare in which aggression and courage in battle were valued traits. Homer himself tells about this ''Age of Heroes,'' this time when savage kings' reputations depended on their

A beautifully decorated bronze and gold sword blade, typical of the weapons of the wealthy at the time of the Trojan war. Compare this to the older dagger pictured on page 47.

destruction of other cities. Kings like Agamemnon, who busied himself fighting and plundering the region around Troy for nine years before taking that city, were highly revered. As historian Michael Wood points out, in Homer the greatest praise is to be called "a sacker of cities."

So, because of the similarity in the structure of their palaces, archaeologists are certain that these Mycenaeans were indeed the dominating force in the area beginning in about 1600 B.C. Their economy apparently depended on the forced labor of slaves, whom they would acquire in their military exploits. These slaves were required to build the palaces, grow the crops, and do everything else that needed to be done to keep the citadels going, so that the kings could continue their battles. Such an empire must have been large and well organized. But by 1200 B.C. their power seems to have ended.

Could They Read and Write?

In the 1890s many interested archaeologists came to the Athens Museum to see for themselves Schliemann's exciting finds from the graves at Mycenae. One of these archaeologists was an Englishman named Arthur Evans.

Evans was intrigued by the notion that the Mycenaeans had dominated not only mainland Greece, but nearby islands such as Crete as well. Homer had specifically mentioned Knossos, a city in northern Crete, as having contributed many ships and men to the war effort against Troy. In the last part of the nineteenth century there had been a few minor excavations at Knossos which turned up Mycenaean pottery. Schliemann wanted to dig there, but had not been able to get permission. Not until several years later, after Turkish rule ceased in 1899, was the site declared available. This time it was Arthur Evans, not Heinrich Schliemann, who would be uncovering secrets of the past.

Sir Arthur Evans, the prominent scholar who came after Schliemann and added to the discoveries about Troy.

Early Phoenician	Early Hebrew (cursive)	Moabite	Phoenician
✗	✗	✗	✗
ϑ	ϑ	ϑ	ϑ
٦	٦	٦	٦
△	٩	△	٩
⅂	⅂	⅂	⅂
Υ	⅄	Υ	٦
I	=	I	I
▤	▱	▯	▯
⊕	ϲ	⊗	⊗
⅄	⅂	⅄	⅃
↓	⅄	⅄	⅄
↙	⅃	⅃	⅃
٤	⅄	⅂	⅄
⅂	⅄	⅄	⅄
≢	ϼ	≢	≢
O	O	O	O
٦	⅃	⅃	⅃
	ⅈ	⅄	⅄
	Υ	φ	φ
٩	۹	◁	◁
W	w	W	W
+	✗	✗	✝✗

Evans believed the Mycenaean civilization, with its ability to dominate the prehistoric world as completely as it had, must have used a written language. At least, he was sure, they needed some system of bookkeeping for all the rations needed to feed their people. How else could they have kept track of slaves, of trade with other people, and of items confiscated in their numerous wars?

Evans's theory contradicted the ideas of his day. Scholars knew that the prehistoric Greeks had borrowed an alphabet from Phoenicia around 800 B.C. Yet he was suggesting that this ancient people, predecessors of the classical Greeks, had a written language several hundred years earlier. If that had been the case, why hadn't that written language continued? Was he saying that these prehistoric people, the Mycenaeans, were more advanced than the Greeks who came after them?

To say that the ancestors of a given people were more warlike, more aggressive in trade, even more wealthy is one thing. But to maintain that these people could read and write while their descendants were illiterate defied logic. How could a civilization lose its literacy? Scholars and specialists in linguistic

Here, two versions of the Phoenician alphabet are compared to other ancient written languages.

This lovely, double-handled vase was found in Troy II.

history were intrigued by the notion, but they demanded proof. Could Evans come up with hard evidence showing that there had been such a language?

Evans knew that if he could find such evidence it would not only satisfy scholars interested in the development of ancient languages, it would shed more light on the Mycenaeans. Remember, the Trojan War was hailed by Homer as a heroic effort of the prehistoric Greeks, these Mycenaeans that Schliemann and his successors had been tracking in the 1870s. The Mycenaeans were the key to unraveling this ancient mystery. Schliemann had demonstrated that they had existed, and he and his followers had pinpointed Troy, the scene of the Mycenaeans' most famous battle. That was a strong beginning, yet Evans wanted to keep searching for more clues about the Mycenaeans and their long-ago empire. The more Homer's words could be supported by hard facts, the more believable Homer would be as a historical source.

Clues that Point to Crete

Evans's curiosity was piqued even further when he discovered some odd little stones in an Athens antique shop. The stones were actually ancient seals, once used to stamp an impression on wax or lead. These seals were engraved with what looked like some kind of writing. Evans could not be sure, so he asked the store owner about their origin.

He was told that the seals came from Crete where they had been found in great supply. Known as "milkstones," these little three- or four-sided stones were thought to be good luck charms, and were worn by many of the women in Crete to ensure a healthy supply of mother's milk.

"Though Homer's account of it may not be completely reliable, the Trojan war did nevertheless take place. It is an historical fact."

French author Robert Flaceliere, *A Literary History of Greece*

"Homer's Trojan War . . . must be evicted from the history of the Greek Bronze Age."

British author Moses Finley, *The World of Odysseus*

Ancient seals used to sign letters and documents. The ones Arthur Evans discovered in an Athens antique shop were engraved with a mysterious ancient form of writing that piqued his curiosity.

Now, in 1900, having bought the Knossos site, Evans eagerly began excavations to see if he could find evidence of ancient Mycenaean writing. Within one week he and his crew hit ancient walls. He assumed at first that the structure would prove to be another grim citadel in the style of the other Bronze Age buildings Schliemann had unearthed on the Greek mainland. What he realized as more of the structure was unearthed was that he had come upon a palace like none he had ever seen. It surpassed the Mycenaean citadels in size and sheer elegance, yet it was centuries older! This, it seemed, was a civilization that until that day had been completely unknown. Who were these people? What did they call themselves?

The Minoans

Evans estimated that the palace had first been built around 2000 B.C., although, like the site at Hissarlik, it had been rebuilt several times. Later, more sophisticated radiocarbon dating techniques supported

A sketch of the ancient palace at Knossos, a sophisticated and complex royal city.

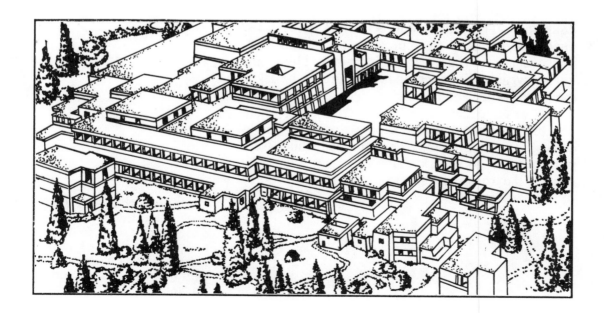

Evans's estimate. These early Bronze Age people were living in luxury and splendor hundreds of years before the Mycenaeans rose to power on the mainland. He dubbed the civilization *Minoan*, because of an ancient Greek legend about Crete.

This legend told of a mighty kingdom on the island of Crete, ruled by King Minos. Minos had a son called the Minotaur, who was half-man and half-bull. The Minotaur lived beneath the huge palace of his father, in a confusing series of winding passageways called a *labyrinth*. Every seven years, so the legend said, King Minos demanded that seven maidens and seven young men be sent from Athens on the mainland. These unfortunates would be offered as a sacrifice to the horrible Minotaur.

This practice continued for years until a brave young Greek named Theseus sailed for Crete with the victims. Aided by Minos's daughter, he found his way through the complex labyrinth, killed the Minotaur, and rescued his companions.

Theseus and the Minotaur in the ancient labyrinth.

The palaces at the time of Troy and Mycenae were elaborately decorated. This is the throne room in the Knossos palace.

> "Beautiful frescoes . . . uncovered by Schliemann in Mycenaean ruins are identical with those found by Sir Arthur Evans in Crete. This leaves no doubt that the Cretans were Mycenae's cultural teachers."
>
> Author I.G. Edmonds, *The Mysteries of Troy*

> "The premise of continuity of race and culture [between Mycenae and Crete] was particularly dubious."
>
> Author Michael Wood, *In Search of the Trojan War*

So, in the early years of the twentieth century Arthur Evans was slowly easing his way through these ancient ruins. As the excavation proceeded, Evans was discovering more about this ancient palace. It covered almost seven acres in the hills of Knossos. There were several levels, and hundreds of rooms. There were many storerooms within the palace, as well as airy, open rooms for musicians, sculptors, and wood-workers. Some of the food-storage rooms contained immense pots—astonishingly enough, still full of beans and grain! There was a sophisticated water drainage system with a remarkably modern indoor plumbing setup. The walls were plastered and decorated with beautiful paintings.

Yet nowhere were there any fortifications or strong walls for defense. These people must have been completely secure. They must have had no enemies to fear.

The Culture of the Bull

The Minoans' artistic abilities, discovered during Evans's excavations at Knossos, are unique. Everywhere there were paintings and frescoes [pictures painted on wet plaster] depicting scenes from nature. Noticeably absent were any pictures like the Mycenaean images of brave warriors, armed with bronze-tipped spears. The paintings Evans unearthed show joyful Minoan men and women dancing and engaging in sports.

One image which is consistently repeated in the art of these ancient people is that of the bull. The head of a bull adorns necklaces, rings, and goblets. Whether the bull is at all tied to the legend of the Minotaur is not known. What *is* known, however, is that one of the favorite pastimes of the Minoans was the sport of bull-leaping. Evans found a multitude of statues and paintings showing a bull charging while a boy or girl somersaulted over its back. Some scholars have speculated on the difficulty and danger of such a sport and have suggested that this was more of a dance. Perhaps,

The Queen's sitting room at Knossos.

The bull was a favorite image on objects of all kinds in the Minoan civilization. Here is a beautiful gold cup found at Mycenae.

Was Minoan bull dancing a well-planned performance or a dangerous competition like modern Spanish bullfighting?

they say, the bull did not charge in anger, as in a Spanish bullfight, but instead was trained to perform, like a circus animal.

Evans found that the more he learned about this ancient civilization, the more he admired the love of life that seemed to radiate from their art and their building style. What possible connection did these people have with the warlike Mycenaeans?

The Mycenaean Connection

Ironically, in trying to understand what ended the lovely and peaceful civilization at Knossos, Evans found one of the puzzle pieces he was looking for—the connection between the Mycenaeans and the Minoans. He had found an abundance of pottery throughout the site, some of which dated back more than three thousand years before Christ. By studying the style of the pottery and other artifacts, he could get an idea of the history of the Minoan empire.

Evans was able to show that the Minoan civilization was thriving in 2000 B.C. The Minoans were a seafaring people who traded extensively with their neighbors in the ancient world. Their style of pottery and jewelry, even their architecture, was sought after and imitated—sought after especially, as it turns out, by the Mycenaeans. Cheaply-made copies of Minoan

pottery have been found among the ruins of Mycenae, Tiryns, and other strongholds on the mainland. To modern archaeologists there definitely appeared to have been trade between the two peoples.

Destruction by Earthquake

The ancient Minoans were struck by tragedy somewhere around 1500 B.C. A violent earthquake and volcanic eruption on the nearby island of Thera destroyed most of Crete. Thera's whole center disappeared completely into the sea; more than 100 feet of volcanic ash covered what was left above sea level. As a point of comparison, the famous volcanic eruption of Krakatoa in Indonesia in 1883 left no more than sixteen inches of ash. In that eruption, 36,000 people were drowned along nearby coasts from the

"The Great Excavation," an etching published in an 1891 issue of *Scientific American*. It shows Schliemann's work very much in progress. Sophie is at the bottom center.

At Mycenae, Arthur Evans found many clay tablets, similar to the one in this picture, covered with unusual writing. This tablet has been engraved with Linear B.

resulting tidal waves. The force of the explosion could be heard in Australia 2,000 miles away! Certainly the volcano at Thera, which is five times larger than Krakatoa, must have resulted in massive loss of life.

No wonder, then, the Minoans were never able to recover from the disaster. The palace was rebuilt, Evans found, but not in the same beautiful way. The building style was much less open. The rooms were smaller and darker. Knossos was overrun by another group of people who took advantage of the devastation and the destruction. They aggressively moved in, bringing their style of architecture with them. Evans could identify the invaders by the pottery and artifacts they brought with them to Knossos.

They were Mycenaeans.

Cryptic Clay Tablets

Throughout the ruins of the palace, and elsewhere on the island of Crete, many clay tablets were found. On them were what appeared to be two very old types of writing, both similar to that on the seal stones that Evans had seen in the Athens antique shop.

Evans found that he could detect differences in the alphabet symbols, although it was easy to see that they were related. Most of the symbols were a sort of squiggly, cursive style of picture writing. The earlier of the two, which he called Linear A, must have been used by the Minoan scribes starting about 1900 B.C. He could identify more than seventy-five different symbols, although he had no idea what they meant. As yet, no one has been able to decipher Linear A except for a few number symbols. Scholars think that the tablets are inventories of livestock and grain, records needed to keep a thriving civilization going.

The second type of writing, called Linear B, was far more interesting to archaeologists, because it was used after the fall of the Minoans. More than 400,000 clay tablets in Linear B script were found in the palace at Knossos. It was a system of writing based on the

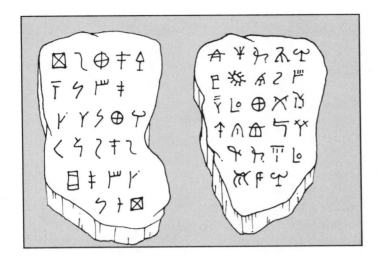

Linear A and Linear B are similar but not identical. Although discovered almost 100 years ago, neither was deciphered until the 1950s.

earlier Linear A, but there were more symbols, eighty-seven in all. The clay tablets inscribed with Linear B date from the period 1450-1400 B.C. It seemed to Evans, based on this information, that Linear B might have been the written language of the Mycenaeans. But what did the Linear B tablets say? They were, to Evans and scores of linguists, incomprehensible.

Another Piece of the Puzzle

Because there was no known language to compare Linear A and Linear B to, scientists thought it might be impossible to decipher them. Normally linguists try to locate a document called a *bilingual* which gives the same information in the unknown language and in a familiar one. For instance, scholars were able to translate the ancient hieroglyphs of Egypt by using the Rosetta Stone, which was imprinted with two known languages—as well as with hieroglyphs.

So for years Linear B went untranslated, a strange code from the prehistoric Bronze Age. Arthur Evans, meanwhile, continued his study of the Minoans and the Mycenaeans, occasionally lecturing on his finds.

It was at one of these lectures that a fourteen-year-old boy named Michael Ventris heard about the

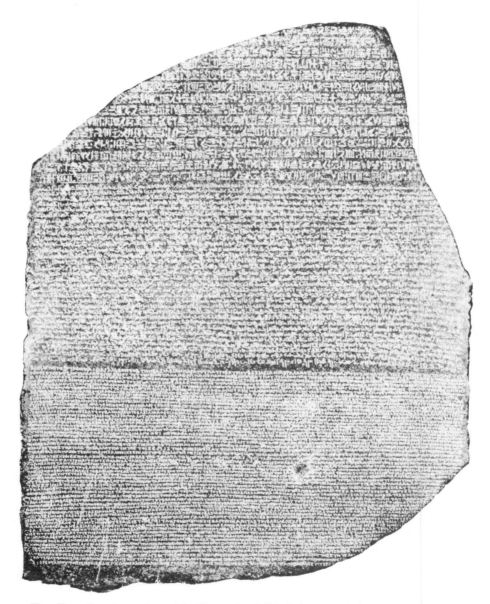

The Rosetta stone, found in Egypt in 1799. It is one of the most famous multilingual stones. It has the same information written in three different languages—Egyptian hieroglyphs, demotic (another ancient Egyptian script), and Greek. Because Greek was known, scholars were able to compare and eventually decipher hieroglyphs for the first time.

mysterious language. Even at the age of fourteen, it was clear that Ventris had a gift for learning languages. He had taught himself Polish at age six; at age seven he bought a book in German about ancient Egyptian hieroglyphics. And this Linear B about which Evans lectured—this sounded like an exciting puzzle. He vowed that someday he would solve it.

Ventris grew up to be a talented architect, but he never outgrew his interest in code breaking and cryptograms. After World War II, Ventris sent a detailed questionnaire to those scholars who were working on Linear B. He was an amateur, they said to themselves, but why not answer his questions, the more the merrier. He began working, trying to find a pattern in the picture writing.

He worked with three very complicated grids that showed which symbols shared consonants and which shared the same vowels. He noted the frequency with which symbols occurred. He looked for similarities in other languages such as Etruscan and Hittite. The fact that there were eighty-eight different symbols confused him. That was far too many for an alphabet, yet far too few for a system of hieroglyphics. Nothing seemed to work.

A Stunning Announcement

He tried thinking of the eighty-eight symbols as syllables, and he began shuffling them around to see if there were some kind of pattern. Finally, in 1951, as a guest on a BBC radio talk show concerning Evans's work, Ventris stunned listeners by announcing that he had *cracked* the code for the language. Linear B was an ancient form of Greek! The syllable theory had been correct, and he was able to prove his theory when Carl Blegen sent him a newfound tablet from an excavation site at Pylos. Could Ventris translate it? Ventris could. The tablet contained some information about a three-legged pot, called a tripod.

"We are convinced that the Mycenaean culture was literate since we have dug up tablets and other objects of clay inscribed with its writing."

Rhys Carpenter, Professor Emeritus of Classical Archaeology at Bryn Mawr College, *Folk Tale, Fiction and Saga in the Homeric Epics*

"The fact is that as yet we know too little about the nature and extent of literacy in Mycenaean kingdoms."

Author Michael Wood, *In Search of the Trojan War*

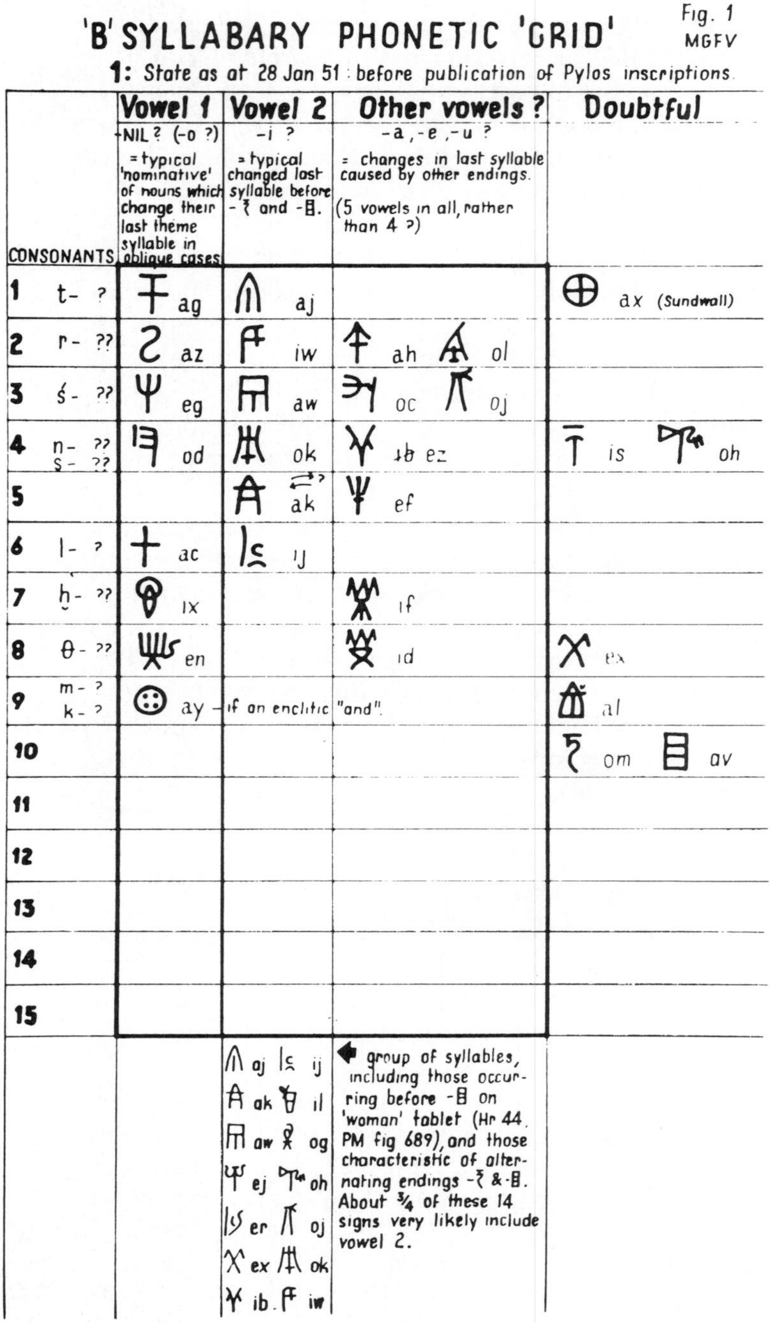

'B' SYLLABARY PHONETIC 'GRID'

Fig. 1
MGFV

1: State as at 28 Jan 51: before publication of Pylos inscriptions.

CONSONANTS	Vowel 1 -NIL? (-o?) = typical 'nominative' of nouns which change their last theme syllable in oblique cases	Vowel 2 -i? = typical changed last syllable before -ꞵ and -ꞵ.	Other vowels? -a,-e,-u? = changes in last syllable caused by other endings. (5 vowels in all, rather than 4?)		Doubtful	
1 t- ?	⊤ ag	⋀ aj			⊕ ax (Sundwall)	
2 r- ??	Ƨ az	Ƒ iw	⇞ ah	⋀ ol		
3 ś- ??	Ψ eg	⊞ aw	⋺ oc	⋔ oj		
4 n- ?? s- ??	⧢ od	⋕ ok	�y ib ez		⊤ is	oh
5		⋀ ak	Ψ ef			
6 l- ?	✝ ac	⋳ ij				
7 h- ??	◉ ix		⋇ if			
8 θ- ??	ⵖ en		⋇ id		⋋ ex	
9 m- ? k- ?	⊡ ay	-if an enclitic "and".			⍟ al	
10					ꟻ om	⊟ av
11						
12						
13						
14						
15						

⋀ aj | ⋳ ij
⋀ ak | ⵫ il
⊞ aw | ꝗ og
Ψ ej | ⵣ oh
⵵ er | ⋔ oj
⋋ ex | ⋕ ok
⋇ ib | Ƒ iw

◄ group of syllables, including those occurring before -ꞵ on 'woman' tablet (Hr 44, PM fig 689), and those characteristic of alternating endings -ꞵ & -ꞵ. About ¾ of these 14 signs very likely include vowel 2.

Michael Ventris was the first to decipher Linear B. This is a sample from his grid system.

The Ventris system worked, and Ventris was hailed by the academic world, almost without exception, as a genius.

The content of practically every tablet was dull; lists of palace records, slaves, and supplies. But one of the most important pieces to the puzzle of whether Homer's poems could have been based on fact was the source of the language itself. There had been two languages found at Knossos, Linear A and Linear B. Evans had known they were related, but they were different, too. Linear A was the Minoans' own language dating from about 1900 B.C. But Linear B, used after the fall of the Minoans, was undeniably a Greek version of Linear A. The Mycenaeans, who had moved in after the earthquake rocked the Minoans, who Homer claimed had waged war against the city of Troy, *were* Greek. More and more Homer's poems looked as though they were based on fact after all.

Six

Was Homer's Story True?

The two participants of a long-ago legendary war have now been identified as real civilizations. As historian Raymond Everett writes, "there is no responsible work showing anything to the contrary." There was an ancient city of Troy (although not much has been learned yet about the Trojans themselves), and there did exist an ancient race of Greeks that scholars call Mycenaeans. The two peoples lived at the same time in history. But is it likely, or even possible, that they could have engaged in war? The abduction of Helen makes for exciting reading, but scholars think that there must have been other motives for a ten-year war.

Archaeologists have found evidence that Mycenaeans had visited Troy often in the fourteenth century B.C. Trade was probably the reason for the visits. Many Mycenaean products found their way into the city; among them were arrowheads, marble sword pommels (handles), daggers made of bronze, and lots of pottery.

Homer mentions more than once that the Trojans were well known as breeders of excellent horses. And since large quantities of horse bones have been excavated at the level of Troy VI, this may very well have been true. In addition to its high-quality horses, Troy was known for both its fishing industry and its fine textiles. Any or all of these could have been bartered for the Mycenaean goods.

Opposite: Historians agree that Troy actually existed, but there is still disagreement about whether or not Homer's tale of Helen and Paris and the rout by the wooden horse really happened. This version of the horse is taken from a vase made centuries after the war would have occurred.

The Trojans traded fine horses and other items with the Mycenaeans and others.

Some scholars have pointed out, too, that an attack by the warlike Mycenaeans on the Trojans would have been right in character. The Mycenaeans' pattern at Knossos may also have worked at Troy: Trade with a neighbor and get to know the lay of the land, become jealous of that neighbor's wealth, and finally, attack that neighbor when the time was right. Just as a natural disaster made the Minoans vulnerable in the fourteenth century, the earthquake at Troy must have exposed the city to the marauding Mycenaeans.

The Trojan Horse

And what about the Trojan horse? It is probably the best-known part of the story. People who can not recall from their school days anything about the war will at least be able to recollect that there was a battle won because of a wooden horse.

According to Homer, the use of the horse to gain access to the city was the plan of Odysseus, a Greek hero known for his cunning. The horse was built by Epeios, who constructed it in such a way that many armed men could crouch inside, weapons and all.

The Trojans' reaction to the horse was mixed. In some accounts of the story, there were people in the city who said that the thing should be destroyed by

This detailed wall painting from around the time of the Trojan war shows a naval expedition. Did the battleships that carried soldiers to Troy resemble these hand-rowed ones?

chopping it into pieces or throwing it over a cliff. In other accounts, citizens were thrilled at the idea of such a magnificent gift and were anxious to bring it inside the walls.

As legend, the horse is an exciting finale to the story, and a good means of one army gaining entrance to the fortress of another. However, to one looking at the Trojan War as history rather than legend, the horse seems to be farfetched. No ancient remains have been discovered that indicate the use of a large wooden horse near Hissarlik; that would be almost too good to be true. Because of the lack of evidence, some have suggested that the horse in the tale of Troy was merely symbolic, more a metaphor than anything else.

Strength or Stealth?

The ancient Greek writer Pausanias, whose writings helped Schliemann locate the grave shafts at Mycenae, wrote that the horse of the story was a huge battering ram. A battering ram, or *siege engine* as it is sometimes called, is a heavy wooden contraption built for the purpose of smashing through an enemy's walls. Pausanias wrote, "Anyone who doesn't think that the Trojans were utterly stupid will have realized that the horse was actually an engineer's device for breaking down the walls."

There are problems with this idea of the battering ram, however. Archaeologists know that battering rams existed and were used quite often in the Near East, especially by the ancient Assyrians. Their armies carried powerful siege engines in the shape of wooden horses; many soldiers were needed to operate them. Yet the earliest use of these Assyrian battering rams has been shown to be in the late twelfth century B.C. There is absolutely no evidence which suggests that battering rams, horse-shaped or otherwise, were being used in the Aegean in the thirteenth century B.C.

Other scholars have pointed out that the theory of the siege engine is quite different from the idea

"The *Iliad* and the *Odyssey*, according to the usual opinion of antiquity and the most modern views of today, were the work of one poet, conventionally called Homer."

Author and Greek scholar H.J. Rose, *A Handbook of Greek Literature*

"I have convinced myself that . . . the *Iliad* which we know was essentially the work of a single author, and our *Odyssey* was the work of a single author; but these two authors could not possibly have been one and the same."

Rhys Carpenter, Professor Emeritus of Classical Archaeology at Bryn Mawr College, *Folk Tale, Fiction and Saga in the Homeric Epics*

behind the horse. It was not military strength, not muscle, that enabled the Greeks to get inside the walls of Troy. Rather, it was trickery and stealth. The story would be far different, they say, without that aspect of it.

One historian has suggested that Homer may have borrowed the general idea of the Trojan horse from the ancient Egyptian tale of Joppa. According to that legend, the city of Joppa was destroyed because of a similar trick. Two foot soldiers carried large gunny sacks slung between two poles into the city. They were allowed inside because they were thought to be carrying gifts. As soon as the soldiers unloaded the first sack, they went back for another load. Of course, there were soldiers concealed inside the gunny sacks. Amazingly, the foot soldiers were able to carry in two hundred warriors! The tale parallels the story of Troy quite nicely, but it is not known whether Homer borrowed the idea from the story of Joppa or not. If he did, the irony of it was a nice touch—a city known for taming wild horses being duped by a phony horse!

Homer as a Historian

This brings us to the subject of Homer as a reliable source for ancient history. Since we think archaeolo-

Was the Trojan horse actually a horse-like battering ram? The one shown is based on an Assyrian wall carving.

gists have found many of the places he mentions in the *Iliad* and the *Odyssey*, such as Troy, Mycenae, and so on, can we assume that he is to be trusted in matters of historic fact?

There have been hundreds of volumes written about Homer describing who he was, where he came from, whether he alone composed both the *Iliad* and the *Odyssey* or whether they were composed by different people. Because Homer lived so long ago, and because the age of Homer is also the age in which the written word was just coming into use in Greece after several centuries of illiteracy, there is a lot of mystery about the poet. The Homeric question, as it is called, will not be our subject here. Rather, let us assume that the *Iliad* and the *Odyssey* were composed by one man, and let us evaluate what we know about his work and the way his poetry was composed.

Homer was an eighth-century B.C. poet who told about events that happened five hundred years earlier, in the thirteenth century B.C. While we know that the Mycenaeans had a written language—Linear B, as Evans called it—we also know that when the Mycenaean dynasty in Greece fell in about 1200 B.C.,

The city of Troy was known for its trade in horses. Here, on a fragment from a vase, the hero Achilles is shown with horses.

Stories say that the city of Joppa was destroyed by a trick as effective as the Trojan horse.

People have debated for centuries: Who was Homer? Was he one writer or several? Did he write fact or fiction? Even today, the answers to these questions are unknown.

Opposite page: A modern "Trojan horse" erected near Troy.

their written language disappeared. For four hundred years, Greece was an illiterate society.

Oral History

So where did Homer get the information about the Trojan War on which he based his poems? He didn't make it all up: The work of Schliemann, Evans, Dörpfeld, and others has shown that much of what he told about really occurred. He certainly could not have studied it or read eyewitness accounts from the Mycenaean age since there were no written records preserved from that time. The obvious answer seems to be that he based his story on tales he listened to. Those tales were based on tales from an earlier poet, and those in turn from an even earlier poet. This is called the *oral tradition*, and it explains how it is possible for a poet to accurately describe events that happened centuries before and at the same time keep thousands of lines of verse straight in his mind.

Scholars know that such as feat is possible, for there are parallels in other civilizations. The famous French epic *Song of Roland*, for example, was written in the twelfth century A.D., but the events described in the poem actually took place in 778. By studying poems composed in the oral tradition, literary scholars have found that many historical facts are accurately preserved. Though a poem may be *based* quite solidly in historical fact, however, such poetry commonly contains exaggerations, distortions, even deliberate misinformation.

Most of the poems in the oral tradition are thrilling adventures of cultural heroes, usually warriors. Indeed, one of the functions of the oral tradition is to keep alive the memories of such heroes. *Beowulf*, for example, tells of the brave deeds of an ancient Anglo-Saxon hero. The oral poet may base the story on a real chain of events. Yet any mention of a hero's weaknesses or frailties would detract from the tale. Often, then, the poet simply changes the story to keep

the hero unblemished. This is one of the options, or licenses, of the poet that does not extend to the historian.

Poetic Tradition

Milman Parry was a linguistic scholar in the 1920s who documented the way the oral tradition works in poetry. He studied the techniques of modern oral poets in Yugoslavia and other parts of the world. Parry learned there are two ways of transmitting a lengthy poem from one generation to the next. The first is for one poet to commit the poem to memory, to hear it word for word again and again until he or she can virtually "play it back" perfectly. This method was used in India to pass down long prayers: Generations of oral poets committed the prayers to memory until they were finally written down hundreds of years later.

The second way long poems have been handed down in illiterate societies is by a system of formulas. These formulas are stock phrases that the poet has on hand—some long, some very short, depending on the need. In the poems of Homer, for instance, Odysseus may be described as "much-endearing Odysseus," and the goddess Athena is always "Athene with her bright eyes snapping." Achilles is either "swift-footed Achilles" or "Achilles, the son of Peleus," depending on the number of syllables Homer needed to make the rhythm of the line come out right.

Historian John Chadwick has pointed out distinct advantages in this formula system. One is that the listener can more easily concentrate on the poem being sung or spoken when he or she is not distracted by hundreds of different references to the same character. The poets telling the stories also have an advantage using these formula phrases. By storing in their memories groups of lines, they do not waste time deciding how to describe something or someone. They always have a second or two to organize the next part of the story, and that can make a lot of difference in the continuity and smoothness of delivery.

It is easy to see why a poem composed in the oral tradition can potentially become monotonous. Because of the constant repetition, the job of the poet is to enliven and embellish the tale, adding factual details to keep it interesting and fresh. In this embellishment the poet leaves his or her marks on the telling of the poem. There are many of these marks in both the *Iliad* and the *Odyssey* that are clues to the accuracy of Homer's historical information.

For example, Homer mentions one of the warriors wearing a particular type of helmet. It was made of ox-hide and decorated on the outside with the tusks of a boar. The helmet was very thick, and it fastened under the chin with a strap. Such helmets were not in use in Homer's day, nor is it likely that any would have survived intact from the Bronze Age to the eighth century B.C. The very detailed description from the *Iliad*, however, matches that of helmets from the thirteenth and fourteenth centuries B.C. that have recently been found on the Greek mainland. (Incidentally, such a helmet must have been very valuable to its owner. Archaeologists estimate that between forty and eighty pairs of tusks were needed to make one helmet!) This would seem to point to a piece of information traveling hundreds of years through generations of oral poets and arriving whole and undamaged.

It is important to remind ourselves, however, that a poet is not a historian, that he or she is concerned not as much with historical accuracy as with human values and emotions. Forcing the poetry to stand up to cold, hard facts detracts from the poet's central purpose. On the other hand, the fact that Homer has been proven reliable in some cases encourages scholars and historians. They would welcome another credible source of information about the Trojan War, an event that until the nineteenth century was dismissed as only legend.

Helmets like this have been found among the remains at Troy. They are made of oxhide covered with slices of boar tusk.

Seven

What Happened to the Heroic Age?

What happened to the victorious Mycenaeans after the siege of Troy? Their civilization appears to have collapsed completely very soon thereafter.

Some scholars have suggested that the Mycenaeans spread themselves too thin, that they simply attempted to do too many things at once. From Mycenaean pottery and weapons found in Cyprus, we know that in addition to overtaking Crete and Troy, these Greeks went eastward. Their travel to Cyprus was important because it gave them a source for the large quantities of copper that they needed to manufacture their weapons. They also ventured as far north as the Cornish coast of Britain to obtain tin.

Another problem was that the Mycenaean empire in Greece was top-heavy: All of the wealth belonged to the king and his army. Very little filtered down to the common men and women who kept the kingdom working. All this wealth had to come either from trade with other societies or from war. As Michael Wood writes, "Both the labor force and the means of coercion could only be sustained by trade or violence; a truly vicious circle." From treasure buried with dead royalty to priceless artifacts used in the palaces (Linear B tablets go into great detail about the ornate furniture

According to Homer, the fall of Troy was accompanied by untold violence, death, and destruction. In this drawing, based on a painting by Cornelius, the Trojan horse looms quietly in the background.

Earthquakes and other natural disasters have contributed to the fall of once-great civilizations. Here, the treasury of the Mycenaean citadel lies in ruins.

demanded by kings), an enormous amount of wealth was needed to sustain the upper class and keep the whole empire going. Add to this the stress of constant wars—100,000 men were involved in the Trojan War alone—and there was a strong danger to the stability of the Mycenaeans.

The Collapse

Around 1250 B.C. there was widespread destruction to the palaces and citadels of the Mycenaeans. They were burned, robbed, and finally destroyed. What happened is not yet known. Archaeologists are certain only that the looted and burned palaces were never rebuilt. Dismal little shacks were later built near the sites of the citadels, but their inhabitants lived on a much poorer scale than their predecessors.

Some scholars point to the legends of strife within royal families—the Mycenaeans were well known for internal power struggles. So perhaps the empire crumbled from within. Also a possibility are raids by other tribes. Some of the Linear B tablets dating to the end of the Mycenaean empire mention that "troops are carefully guarding the coastal regions."

Another point to consider is that natural disasters may have preceded the end of the heroic age described by Homer. Many researchers are examining the possibilities of drought and famine in the mid-thirteenth century B.C. Such a drought might have caused wide economic collapse and could have easily weakened the empire so that it was vulnerable to an outside enemy.

The Decline of Greece

Whatever the cause, the archaeological remains of the time show very little in the way of an organized society after the time of the Trojan siege. The pottery excavated from this period shows diversity, which would seem to indicate that small bands or tribes of people were fending for themselves. Greek trade with other people in the ancient world stopped entirely. All of the luxuries of the Mycenaean age were gone. Slaves, farming, trade, weapons; all of these had been controlled and regulated by the kings. The written language, used by royal scribes in Mycenaean palaces, disappeared completely. With the collapse of the kings came the collapse of the whole society.

The next four hundred years were frightening times. Called the Dark Ages, this time period in Greece was one of fear and decline. Accounts by ancient Greek writers such as Thucycides as well as archaeological excavations have shown that most Greek towns were looted and destroyed. In place of the towering Mycenaean palaces, says historian Emily

"The town of Mycenae was destroyed by the Argives after the Persian Wars."

Professor J.P. Mahaffy, quoted in *The Mysteries of Homer's Greeks*

"Historically, no one knows what brought about the fall. But if we study the legends, it becomes clear that the fall of Mycenae came about from internal disturbances."

Author I.G. Edmonds, *The Mysteries of Homer's Greeks*

Vermeule, rose "flimsy and squalid buildings." Roving bands of robbers and killers took advantage of the chaos. By 1100 B.C. the population of mainland Greece was about one-tenth of what it had been a century before. Archaeologists find that important crafts and skills were completely lost during this time. No longer were people able to carve ivory, build with large blocks of cut stone, or produce beautiful jewelry. This knowledge had evidently vanished with the palace artisans. An era had ended.

Opposite page: Killing, looting, and destruction led to the Greek dark ages.

Epilogue

The Search Continues

Opposite page: Homer's epic tale of the Trojan war has lived in the world's imagination for more than two thousand years.

The story of the Trojan War is remarkable, but the detective work necessary to prove that it really happened was no less heroic than the exploits of Homer's heroes. Heinrich Schliemann's blind faith in Homer's authenticity, Arthur Evans's careful scholarship, the work of Wilhelm Dörpfeld and Carl Blegen, and the painstaking puzzle-solving of Michael Ventris all have brought a whole era of prehistory to light.

Not every question has been answered. No one knows if there actually was a Helen or a Hector or an Achilles. These are details that may never be known. But modern research goes on, archaeologists continue to sift through the ancient sands of Greece and Turkey, looking for pieces to complete the puzzle. For now, it is enough to know that there once existed a great and noble age before recorded history began, a time of skilled craftspeople, enormous wealth, and military power, when heroes ventured far from home across the Aegean Sea.

Books for Further Exploration

American Heritage editors, *Mysteries of the Past.* New York: American Heritage, 1975.

Arnold C. Brackman, *The Dream of Troy.* New York: Mason and Lipscomb, 1974.

John Chadwick, *Decipherment of Linear B.* New York: Cambridge University Press, 1958.

John Chadwick, *The Mycenaen World.* New York: Cambridge University Press, 1976.

Arthur Cotterell, *The Minoan World.* New York: Charles Scribner's Sons, 1979.

Alexander Eliot, *The Horizon Concise History of Greece.* New York: American Heritage, 1972.

Christopher Fagg, *Ancient Greece.* New York: Warwick, 1979.

Reynold Higgins, *The Archaeology of Minoan Crete.* New York: Henry Z. Walck, 1973.

John Ellis Jones, *Ancient Greece.* New York: Warwick, 1983.

Richmond Lattimore, *The Iliad of Homer.* Chicago: University of Chicago Press, 1951.

J.V. Luce, *Homer and the Heroic Age.* New York: Harper and Row, 1975.

Robert Payne, *The Gold of Troy.* New York: Funk & Wagnalls, 1959.

Carl Schuchhardt, *Schliemann's Discoveries of the Ancient World*. New York: Avenel, 1979.

Lord William Taylour, *The Myceneans*. London: Thames and Hudson, 1964.

R.J. Unstead, editor, *See Inside: An Ancient Greek Town*. New York: Warwick, 1979.

Michael Wood, *In Search of the Trojan War*. New York: Facts on File, 1985.

Index

Achilles, 20, 21, 36, 38, 41, 96, 104
Aeneas, 21, 23
Agamemnon, 19, 24, 56, 58, 60, 68, 69, 73
Alexander the Great, 21
Aphrodite, 17-18
archaeology, 26, 35, 39, 42-50, 60, 65
Assyrians, 91
Athena, 17-18, 21, 23, 96

Blegen, Carl, 66, 67-69, 85, 104
Bretano, E., 52
Bunarbashi (Turkey), 33-39

Caesar, Julius, 23
Calvert, Frank, 39, 42
Chadwick, John, 96
Crete, 73, 75, 76, 77, 80, 82, 87, 90

Dörpfeld, Wilhelm, 64, 67, 94, 104

Eris, 17-18
Evans, Arthur, 73-80, 82, 83, 85, 93, 104
Everett, Raymond, 88

Gell, William, 59-60
Gladstone, William, 63
Greeks, 10-13, 19-21, 23, 56-64
  alphabet of, 16, 74, 82-87, 94
  ancient society of, 56, 58, 101
  decline of ancient, 98, 100, 101, 103

Hector, 14, 20, 36, 104
Helen, 18-19, 52, 88, 104
Hera, 17-18
Herodotus, 21
Hissarlik (Turkey), 39-56, 60, 64, 76, 91
  see also Troy
Homer, 14-17, 19, 20-21, 23, 24-25, 31, 56,
66, 69, 70, 72, 75, 87, 90, 92-93, 96-97, 101, 104
  as reliable, 66, 68, 69, 87, 92-97
  as sacrilegious, 24
  poetry of, 16, 19, 20-21, 23, 24-25, 33, 38,
    39, 50, 56, 66, 69, 70, 72, 75, 87
  questioned, 24, 25

Iliad, 14, 17, 21, 23, 24, 35, 36, 42, 56, 58,
70, 93, 97

Jebb, R.C., 52
Joppa, 92

Knossos (Crete), 73, 76, 78, 80, 82, 87, 90

Leake, William, 59-60
Lechevalier, Jean Baptiste, 34
Linear A and B, 82-87, 93, 98, 100, 101
Lord, Albert, 16

Maclaren, Charles, 39
Menelaus, 18
Minoans, 76-87
  art of, 78, 80
  civilization of, 77, 78
    decline, 81-82
  connection with Mycenaeans, 80-81, 82
  language of, 82-87
Minos, 77
Minotaur, 77
Müller, Max, 63
Mycenae (Greece), 19, 24, 56, 58-62, 69, 73
  treasures of, 60-64, 76
Mycenaeans, 70-76, 80, 82-87, 90, 98
  characteristics of, 72-73, 90, 98
  citadel of, 70, 72, 76
  decline of, 98, 100
  language of, 74, 76

trade of, 88

Odysseus, 14, 23, 90, 96
Odyssey, 14, 17, 21, 23, 24, 35, 56, 93, 97
oral tradition, 16, 94, 96-97

Paris, 17-18, 20
Parry, Milman, 16, 96
Pausanias, 60, 91
Plato, 21
pottery, as clue to civilizations, 65, 67, 80, 101
Priam, 44, 50, 52, 67

Romans, 21-23

Schliemann, Heinrich, 25, 26-33, 35-66, 69,
  70, 72, 73, 75, 76, 91, 94, 104
  archaeological methods of, 42-53, 60
  critics of, 31, 46, 52-53, 63
  defenders of, 53-54, 63
  discoveries of, 39-56, 60-62, 70, 76, 91, 94
  influence of, 26
  language abilities of, 30-33
  youth of, 28-30
Schliemann, Sophie, 42, 51, 64
Stephani, Rudolf, 52

Theseus, 77
Trojan horse, 10, 50, 90-91
Trojan war
  as myth, 23-24, 33-34, 56
  cause of, 17-20
  described, 10-13, 17-20, 28, 56, 68, 88, 100
  existence of, 20, 25, 26, 56, 58, 69, 88, 97
    Greek belief in, 20-21
    Roman belief in, 21-23
  legends of, 14, 17-20, 25, 33, 56, 97
  see also Homer, poetry of
Trojans, 10-13, 14, 17-21, 26-55
  horses of, 88
Troy, search for, 10, 23-24, 26, 29
  in Bunarbashi, 33-39
  in Hissarlik, 39-41, 60, 64, 65-66
    archaeological methods, 42-54
    cities of, 48-52, 64, 66
    Stone Age settlement of, 47-48

treasures of, 51-53

Ventris, Michael, 83, 85-87, 104
Vermeule, Emily, 103
Virchow, Rudolf, 54

Wood, Michael, 69, 73

Picture Credits

About the Author

Gail Stewart received her undergraduate degree from Gustavus Adolphus College in St. Peter, Minnesota. She did her graduate work in English, linguistics, and curriculum study at the College of St. Thomas and the University of Minnesota. Gail taught English and reading for more than ten years.

She has written twenty-five books for young people, including a six-part series called *Living Spaces*. This is her first Great Mysteries book.

Gail and her husband live in Minneapolis with their three sons, two dogs, and a cat. She enjoys reading (especially children's books) and playing tennis.